Governing NOW

Governing NOW

Grassroots Activism in the National
Organization for Women

Maryann Barakso

Cornell University Press
Ithaca and London

First published 2004 by Cornell University Press
First printing, Cornell Paperbacks, 2004

Printed in the United States of America

Library of Congress Cataloging-in-Publication Data

Barakso, Maryann.
 Governing NOW : grassroots activism in the National Organization for Women / Maryann Barakso.
   p. cm.
 Includes bibliographical references and index.
 ISBN 0-8014-4280-X (cloth : alk. paper)—ISBN 0-8014-
8910-5 (pbk. : alk. paper)
 1. National Organization for Women—History. 2. Women's
rights—United States—History—20th century. I. Title.
 HQ1421.B36 2005
 305.42'06'073—dc22
                          2004010280

Cornell University Press strives to use environmentally responsible suppliers and materials to the fullest extent possible in the publishing of its books. Such materials include vegetable-based, low-VOC inks and acid-free papers that are recycled, totally chlorine-free, or partly composed of nonwood fibers. For further information, visit our website at www.cornellpress.cornell.edu.

Cloth printing   10 9 8 7 6 5 4 3 2 1
Paperback printing   10 9 8 7 6 5 4 3 2 1

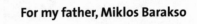

For my father, Miklos Barakso

Contents

Preface

The number and political influence of interest groups in American politics began dramatically increasing in the 1960s. At the same time, scholars largely abandoned earlier approaches to the study of political organizations which examined their internal political systems with an eye to discovering the extent to which their structures fostered representation and participation.[1]

Governing NOW revisits earlier approaches to group behavior. I contend that the history (and the future) of the National Organization for Women (NOW) is most accurately conceived of as a product of the interactions between NOW leaders and members, interactions that take place in the context of a political system formalized by the group during its founding period. NOW's behavior is fundamentally shaped by its political system, or governance structure.

NOW's governance structure shaped the set of organizational goals and tactics (in other words, the "strategic repertoire") deemed legitimate by its leaders and members. When considering potential strategies, leaders of social movement organizations do not necessarily rely solely, or even primarily, on their assessment of the opportunities and resources technically available to them in the political environment. Leaders (and members) evaluate strategic and tactical choices through the prism of their organization's governance system. One of the few benefits a social movement group offers adherents is intangible yet powerful: that of identifying with like-minded individuals in the pursuit of a common purpose.

I maintain that the framework of an organization's collective identity is embedded within its political system. Employing a systematic analytical framework that takes seriously the internal political systems of membership-based voluntary associations contributes to our understanding of a host of questions about such organizations, such as why they choose some goals and tactics over others, why they invest their resources as they do, and why they join or abstain from coalition politics. This framework also offers tools with which to predict a group's long-term viability and political prospects.

In this book, for example, I build on the important findings of political scientist Jane Mansbridge in her book *Why We Lost the ERA*.[2] Mansbridge showed how a proposal that appeared to enjoy widespread support from the public and that rallied masses of activists could nonetheless fail. It faltered, Mansbridge argues, in part due to the fact that most ERA activists were volunteers receiving no tangible benefits from the work they invested in the ratification campaign. In NOW's case, its leaders provided volunteers with an intangible or "purposive" benefit to maintain their motivation by overstating—or allowing others to overstate—the potential impact of the amendment's ratification. But exaggerating the effects of the ERA also encouraged the mobilization of the opposition, eroding its chances of passage.

Yet, not all volunteer organizations working on the ERA ratification drive felt the same need that NOW leaders and members did to emphasize the social, political, and economic changes the amendment would engender. Nor did they all agree on the appropriate tactics to use during the campaign, although the groups commandeered broadly similar resources and were operating in a macropolitical environment with the same opportunities and constraints as NOW.

The exigencies of keeping their members satisfied certainly influenced the tactical choices of all membership groups dedicated to the

ERA campaign. In NOW's case, however, leaders' choices were shaped by the group's particular political structure, one that emphasized the values of being a vanguard, cutting-edge feminist organization that mobilized and empowered grassroots activists. NOW leaders had trouble, when they tried at all, reining in local chapters and members' rhetoric not only because it is difficult to control volunteers but because the organization's principles and practices constrained their ability to do so.

Approach and Methods

This book focuses on strategy choice and change in the National Organization for Women, in part because strategies are so closely linked to organizational identity. Proposed strategy changes tend to instigate internal group debates that bring to light the principles and practices that matter most to group members and leaders. In addition, an organization's ability to change strategies can affect its long-term survival, membership growth, and political power.

Throughout the book I look especially closely at two factors: (1) whether members' statements and actions reflect a knowledge of and interest in the group's guiding principles and decision-making structure, and (2) whether the rhetoric and actions of leaders reflect the influence of the group's governance structure.

Information gleaned from field research, document analysis, and interviews form the basis of this account. The documents analyzed spanned more than three decades of the group's history and included nearly complete sets of national meeting minutes, annual conference reports, national newsletters, and national budgets.[3] I also read every *New York Times* article that mentioned the National Organization for Women between the years 1966 and 2003.

As a participant observer, I attended seven of NOW's annual national membership conferences and one regional conference between the years 1992 and 2003; I also examined transcripts of previous conference plenary sessions. These conferences provided an excellent window into NOW's internal politics, as they constitute the locus of debates among members and between members and leaders regarding the group's official policies, priorities, goals, and tactics. I also examined almost thirty years' worth of official conference guides issued to members at every annual meeting.

To clarify NOW's internal political dynamics and processes, I also conducted open-ended as well as structured in-person interviews ranging from 1.5 to over four hours in duration with a stratified sample of twenty respondents. The sample included current NOW leaders (among them Patricia Ireland and Kim Gandy, the most recent presidents of the organization), founders of the organization, long-time activists and leaders from a variety of geographic regions, and "young feminists" who are relatively new to the organization.

Using these resources, I composed an event history of each period of NOW's development. To verify the reliability and validity of the data, I developed a second chronology derived from secondary sources that described significant events in the external political environment in which the organization operated. These timelines formed the basis of a detailed narrative of each significant event that took place in NOW, which paid particular attention to how the event arose, the reaction of leaders, the reaction of members, and the event's resolution. Using this narrative I created a "case dynamics matrix" that helped generate and corroborate the book's findings about the way NOW's leaders and members responded to and resolved the significant challenges and crises the organization faced.[4]

Finally, I performed a content analysis of several sets of documents, such as board meeting minutes, from which I generated category counts and frequency distributions of words and themes as they appeared over time. This exercise provided insight into the meanings that NOW members and leaders ascribed to and derived from organizational events. I also tabulated frequencies of events such as the numbers and themes of workshops conducted at conferences over the organization's history.

Acknowledgments

I express my profound appreciation to advisers, colleagues, and friends who offered early advice and encouragement on this project at MIT. I am especially grateful to Stephen Ansolabehere, Daniel Kryder, Richard Locke, Kay Lehman Schlozman, Charles Stewart, Richard Valelly, and Elizabeth Wood. I also owe special thanks to Jocelyn Crowley and Kira Sanbonmatsu.

American University's support for its faculty in the form of summer research grants, a University Research Award, and a Junior Faculty Research Leave provided crucial funds and time to finish the manuscript. I warmly acknowledge my colleagues at American, some of whom plowed through entire drafts and others who provided encouraging pats on the back when they were much needed. They include Christine DeGregorio, Jennifer Segal Diascro, Gregg Ivers, Bill Leogrande, Saul Newman, Karen O'Connor, Joe Soss, Patricia Sykes, and Jim Thurber.

Many other very busy scholars, some of whom I have yet to meet personally, lent encouragement, practical advice, and comments on drafts along the way. Among them are Lisa Baldez, Lee Ann Banaszak, Karen Beckwith, Jeffrey Berry, Barbara Burrell, Anne Costain,

Sue Carroll, Mary Hawkesworth, John Green, Mary Fainsod Katzenstein, Eileen McDonagh, Andrew S. McFarland, Jane Mansbridge, David Meyer, Debra Minkoff and Theda Skocpol. The comments of anonymous reviewers, along with editorial assistance from Cornell University Press, also improved the book in important ways.

Without the participation of NOW leaders and activists, many of whom requested anonymity, this book would be very different. I owe particular debts of gratitude to Ivy Bottini, Alice Cohan, Robin Davis, Barbara DiTullio, Kim Gandy, Patricia Ireland, Andrea Lee, Austin Lin, Kris Moody, Judith Meuli, Debra Northart, Susannah Northart, Eleanor Cutri Smeal, Toni Troop, Toni Van Pelt, Lois Galgay Reckitt, Hannah Riddering, Jean Stapleton, Marion Wagner, Jan Welch, and the dozens of activists who patiently and generously answered my countless questions about NOW's inner workings. Many activists I interviewed expressed their longing for NOW's "real story" to be told. I hope that this book rings true to them. *Governing NOW* cannot, nor does it attempt to, describe every significant organizational event or activity. Multiple accounts of NOW's astoundingly rich history should be published, as I expect they will be, by activists and historians in years to come.

As a first-generation American born of working-class Hungarian immigrants, I never dreamed I would earn a doctorate. I attended Barnard College without a penny to my name; to that institution I will forever be grateful. My adviser and very first political science professor at Barnard, Esther Fuchs, insisted I apply to MIT. Her inspiration and confidence in me are largely why I chose to become an academic.

Finally, this book could not have been written without the love of family members, including Miklos Barakso, Ann and Jim Martin, and my sister Elizabeth I. Angelino. My children, Sarah Elisabeth Barakso Martin and Eleanor Ann Martin Barakso, remind me of my blessings every day, and I appreciate their patience during those many weekends when Mom was working on her book. My husband, Larry Martin, has proved unwavering in his belief in me since our teenage years, and I thank him with all my heart.

M. B.

Bethesda, Maryland

Abbreviations

AARP   American Association of Retired Persons (former name)

AAUW   American Association of University Women

ACLU   American Civil Liberties Union

BPW   National Federation of Business and Professional
        Women's Clubs

CEA   Constitutional Equality Amendment

COFO   Council of Federated Organizations

CORE   Congress of Racial Equality

C-R   consciousness-raising

CWLU   Chicago Women's Liberation Union

EEOC   Equal Employment Opportunity Commission

ERA   Equal Rights Amendment

LAPAC   Life Amendment Political Action Committee

LWV	League of Women Voters
NAACP	National Association for the Advancement of Colored People
NARAL	National Abortion Rights Action League
NAWL	National Association of Women Lawyers
NCPAC	National Conservative Political Action Committee
NWPC	National Women's Political Caucus
NYRW	New York Radical Women
OR	Operation Rescue
PCSW	President's Commission on the Status of Women
R2N2	Reproduction Rights National Network
SDS	Students for a Democratic Society
SNCC	Student Nonviolent Coordinating Committee
UAW	United Auto Workers
WAC	Women's Action Coalition
WEAL	Women's Equity Action League
WHAM	Women's Health Action and Mobilization
WILPF	Women's International League for Peace and Freedom
WSP	Women's Strike for Peace

Governing NOW

1. Governance Structures and Strategy Choice and Change in Membership Organizations

In the summer of 2000, members of the campus-based Gainesville, Florida, chapter of the National Organization for Women (NOW) staged a protest in Los Angeles. The target of their wrath? NOW itself. Parading their placards in the midst of the organization's annual convention, these young activists protested NOW's apparent failure to invest adequate resources in preserving women's reproductive rights.

NOW's internal political history is punctuated by relatively minor protests over strategic issues like this one, as well as by far more rancorous disputes that threatened to destroy the group entirely. Episodes of intraorganizational discord and political wrangling over strategy choice and change are common features of the internal landscapes of social movement and other membership-based voluntary associations and frequently lead to their demise. Yet students of organizational behavior do not typically give these internal political dynamics a close and systematic examination.

Governing NOW, a case study of the National Organization for Women, explains NOW's strategic history as a product of the group's internal political system. (By strategies, I mean NOW's goals and the tactics it uses to pursue them.) A feminist organization founded in 1966 and claiming more than 500,000 contributing members and five hundred chapters, NOW is one of the most prominent membership-based interest groups in the United States. It remains the largest feminist organization founded during the second wave of the women's movement.

Organizational Governance Structures and the Strategic Development of Groups

By the close of 1971, as I show more fully in chapter 2, NOW leaders and members had solidified the organization's *governance structure*, which is simply a political system described by a group's guiding principles (its goals and values) on the one hand and its formal decision-making process on the other. This political system holds the key to understanding why the group employs some strategies and not others.

NOW's guiding principles incorporated the following commitments: (1) to remain in the vanguard of the women's movement; (2) to be an activist rather than an educational group; (3) to maintain political independence from governmental and political institutions; (4) to focus on a diverse set of issues and tactics; and (5) to mobilize activists at the grass roots. NOW's formal decision making processes provided significant opportunities for member participation and representation.

Resources, Political Opportunities, and Identity

My approach to understanding NOW departs from the norm: relatively few of the many important analyses of social movements and interest groups focus chiefly on the internal dynamics of those organizations.[1] Analyses of voluntary associations pay scant attention to the political history and bureaucracy of the organizations they study.[2]

How are groups typically analyzed, if not through their political systems? Why do standard analytical tools fail to explain the strategic development of the National Organization for Women? Broadly speaking, three analytical hooks dominate studies of both interest and social movement group behavior. One influential way of understanding social movement and interest group activity emerged from the insight that in order to form and function, groups require resources to subsidize the substantial financial and time-related costs of collective action. Organizational leaders figure prominently here, as it is their primary task to collect and maintain the resources necessary to sustain the group.[3] Organizational decisions—regarding goals or tactics, for example—are presumed to be influenced largely by the exigencies of resource management. Such choices are likely to hinge, for example, on the preferences of generous patrons who underwrite the group's activities, or more generally on the need to conserve or attract further resources.[4]

While acknowledging the importance of resources in explaining organizational behavior, later theorists argue that placing resources at the center of organizational life virtually divorces groups from their social and political environment. In doing so, this approach threatens to overlook other powerful influences on organizational behavior. For example, the choices social movement organizations make are linked not only to resource availability but also to the political opportunities available to them at a given time.[5] The state of the economy, the level of competition between political parties, the presence or absence of groups expressing contrary views—all these sociopolitical and economic variables can affect membership organizations and their activities. Situating groups firmly within the political context also brings members back into accounts of organizations as significant participants. Scholars have shown, for example, that critical organizational resources may flow from a group's "indigenous base" rather than primarily from externally situated elites who are sympathetic to the cause, as previously suggested.[6]

The role of identity as it is constructed by organizations constitutes a third, increasingly common, concept that scholars have drawn on to expand our knowledge of membership group behavior.[7] Organizational identities, or "collective belief systems," are integral to the life of membership groups. The coherence and resonance of a group's shared set of values can increase the likelihood that its members remain active supporters, for example. On the other hand, an organization's belief system can also hamper the group's growth, instigate internal conflict, and threaten long-term viability.[8]

Despite the value of each of these conceptual approaches, as I sifted through archives and interview notes and pondered the countless meetings I attended in order to understand NOW's strategic decisions over time, I found that none adequately explained the puzzles that emerged. For example, during NOW's fragile, formative period (1966–71), why did the group vote to support the Equal Rights Amendment (ERA), abortion, and lesbian rights? NOW founders and members knew that each of these positions would prove to be costly ones for the new group in terms of members and money. For example, when it decided to support the ERA, NOW lost its only office space.

Taking into account the sociopolitical context proves more helpful than a focus on resources in making sense of these risky choices. Contrary to the standard accounts, NOW founders sought to avoid what they viewed as the timid, incremental strategies favored by organizations such as the NAACP. They envisioned a "vanguard" organization, which helps explain NOW's early, bold positions. The political context similarly suggests why NOW resolved to support lesbian rights in 1971. The diffusion of the ideas and members of radical women's liberation groups into NOW influenced the group's institutionalization of this policy.

Although the sociopolitical environment between 1966 and 1971 reveals what originally motivated NOW to support these issues, the political context does not adequately explain NOW's continuing commitment to issues on the cutting edge of feminist politics. Political contexts change; by the end of the 1970s many of NOW's founders were no longer deeply involved in the organization, and radical women's liberation groups had largely disbanded.[9] Yet NOW did not, over time, abandon its determination to remain on the leading edge of the feminist movement; indeed, the group regularly takes positions to the left of other prominent feminist organizations today.

The third analytical tool, the concept of collective identity or belief system, seems to provide an easy solution to the puzzle of NOW's sustained commitment to the vanguard. But this approach also raises more questions than it answers. How, exactly, did NOW develop a widely agreed-on belief system during its founding period, one that guides the group's behavior decades later? How are these beliefs transmitted and maintained over time?

Governance Structures

Placing NOW's governance structure at the center of this analysis resolves questions like these by explicitly revealing the group's goals and values along with the rules governing member influence on organizational decision making. Governance structures help define the group's set of legitimate activities, including its tactical repertoire; activities inconsistent with the group's goals and values are unlikely to be seriously considered or pursued.[10] As Marshall Ganz notes, "although organizational form may be a founders' strategic choice, once established, it has a profound influence on subsequent innovation and strategy."[11] Strategies and tactics are reflections of organizational life. They convey information about the priorities and commitments of organizations. Leaders and members use the lens of their group's political system to view their strategic options.[12]

Although guiding principles are clearly influential in organizational life, the other main constituent of a group's governance structure, its formal decision-making processes, are no less significant. These rules determine how representative the group is of its members and the extent to which members may affect organizational decisions. The decisions groups make are influenced by the level of member representation and participation provided by their governance structures. A structure providing multiple channels for member voice and involvement imposes potentially greater constraints on an organization's leaders than a structure that more firmly establishes organizational power in the hands of a small group of leaders.

David Knoke points out that "organizational designs laid down early in an organization's life cycle tend to persist relatively unaltered during subsequent periods when environments may change markedly."[13] Although this observation is largely true of the National Organization for Women, the group also enacted significant changes to its decision-making structure after its founding. A group's political system or governance structure is a dynamic albeit path-dependent one, developing over time as a result of the interactions of participants and the external conditions the group encounters, for example. As with the development of any institution, over time the choices members and leaders make about their group's political system constrain future possibilities. The organizational principles and processes that define member-leader expectations and interactions not only determine how organizations maintain themselves but also affect their future prospects.

Knoke also argues, "The threat of minority control in American associations seems to be severely constrained by pervasive cultural expectations that the membership will retain ultimate authority and influence over collective actions. Egalitarian norms not only integrate members into these institutions, but inoculate the organizations against antidemocratic inclinations." This argument fails to explain why we find considerable variation in the representative and participatory options offered by interest groups in the United States, however.[14]

Refining Explanations of Organizational Development and Behavior

Groups' political systems deserve attention first because they enrich our knowledge of the behavior of membership organizations. Analyzing groups' political structures enhances our ability to ascertain what motivates a group to undertake certain actions as well as what constrains its behavior.

Groups regularly make "irrational" strategic decisions in the pursuit of their political goals—by ignoring obvious political opportunities, for example, or by appearing to invest their organizational resources inefficiently. A deconstruction of a group's political system resolves many of these apparent inconsistencies. For example, NOW's governance structure helps explain why it took the group six years to decide to make the passage of the Equal Rights Amendment a top priority, and it provides the key to understanding why, at the height of the group's activity in electoral politics in 1992, NOW continued to invest scarce resources in such seemingly anachronistic activities as consciousness-raising. Modifying current models of organizational behavior by taking into account groups' internal political lives transforms apparently inexplicable decisions about strategy choice and change into comprehensible ones.

Second, organizations' governance structures provide clues about groups' prospects for growth and survival. Strategic flexibility is one critical factor determining an organization's success and longevity. It is extremely common, however, for groups to fall apart because of clashes over strategy change. In 1968 a handful of NOW members, objecting to the organization's resolution to support abortion rights, abandoned NOW at a crucial juncture to form the Women's Equity Action League (WEAL). Such exoduses can seriously diminish an organization's resources and undermine the morale of the remaining leaders and members. Although NOW survived numerous internal disagreements over strategy change, many other groups have not fared so well—witness the devitalized Congress of Racial Equality (CORE) and the demise of other formerly vibrant groups such as the Chicago Women's Liberation Union (CWLU) and the Reproductive Rights National Network (R2N2). How did NOW manage to navigate these obstacles when others faltered?

The evidence from NOW's case strongly suggests that the internal political dynamics of NOW's founding period, 1966–71, when leaders and members solidified the group's principles and formal decision-making structure, played a crucial role in sustaining the organization during such crises. Organizations' governance structures, in other words, offer clues about the factors that may either strengthen them for a long and healthy future despite the inevitable stumbling blocks or relegate them to a brief moment in time.

NOW's governance structure provides for considerable strategic flexibility and thus contributes to its survival, but it also significantly constrains the organization's future growth and, as a result, its political power. As NOW members became increasingly active in the life of the organization, they exerted more influence on the group's leaders and even its structure. By institutionalizing increased representation for themselves, members simultaneously ensured the group's continued focus on its guiding principles.

Paradoxically, NOW's democratic decision-making structure, when combined with these guiding principles, undermines the organization's ability to appeal to the public and thus to increase its political power. When voluntary associations can claim to represent ever-larger numbers of constituents, their political power is enhanced. NOW's leaders, however, are constrained by their own rank-and-file members from taking positions or pursuing strategies that might attract a broader following. In this book I argue that although NOW activists rapidly transformed NOW into a highly representative and participatory organization, the group's political structure also significantly undercuts its leaders' ability to fulfill its primary goal: to effect political change.

Civic Engagement and Membership Organizations

This research sheds light on the civic roles of NOW and other membership organizations. Some observers of trends in civic engagement are skeptical that meaningful participatory opportunities are available to members of groups despite the ubiquity of politically oriented voluntary associations. Such scholars have argued, for example, that the dominant form of member participation within such groups is check writing.[15] Not surprisingly, Sidney Verba, Kay Lehman Schlozman, and Henry E. Brady found that making financial contributions is less satisfying than becoming involved in more integrative forms of political activity.[16] The mere donation of funds hardly seems to fulfill the requirements of authentic civic engagement, which according to Martha L. McCoy and Patrick L. Scully "implies meaningful connections among citizens and among citizens issues, institutions, and the political system. It implies voice and agency, a feeling of power and effectiveness, with real opportunities to have a say. It implies active participation, with real opportunities to make a difference."[17] Yet, conventional wisdom posits that voluntary associations no longer contribute significantly to the development of what Harry Boyte calls the public's "civic muscle."[18]

On the other hand, the claim that interest groups play an insignificant role in the political engagement of citizens lacks adequate empirical support. Yet analyses of the relationship between interest groups and civic engagement typically hinge on aggregate measures such as the changing density of the group sector, fluctuations in membership levels, and shifts in organizational structure over time (for example, changes in the number of federated groups).[19] These variables reveal little about the political infrastructures of groups despite the fact that this structure is precisely what defines the relationship between members and groups. In fact, numerous studies document the still-powerful connection between associational membership and political engagement.[20] The dissonance between these findings may be resolved, in part, by attending more carefully to the "micropolitics" of such groups. In short, some associations provide their members more, and more meaningful, opportunities for participation or acquisition of civic skills than others.[21]

Members of the National Organization for Women, for example, elect leaders at every level of the organization, including board members and executive officers; many develop their political skills by attending conferences and workshops at the state, regional, and national levels. On the other hand, members of AARP (formerly known as the American Association of Retired Persons) enjoy no voting rights at all. Such variations are clearly a consequence of these organizations' guiding principles and decision-making processes.

Plan of the Book

NOW's founding period spans the years 1966–71. In chapter 2 I analyze the role members, as well as leaders, played in the institutionalization of the group's governance structure. The group's earliest goals and tactical choices are examined in chapter 3. In chapter 4 I trace NOW leaders' halting progress toward building an ERA campaign, noting activists' apparent reluctance to invest heavily in the drive. Members feared that the ratification campaign would undermine NOW's principles and structure. In chapter 5 I show that even during NOW's full-blown ERA "emergency campaign" (1978 through 1982), members of the organization expressed many reservations about this narrow focus and the tactics NOW was using to pursue it. The group's leaders continued to adhere to its guiding principles by addressing other issues even as they sought the constitutional amendment's passage.

In chapter 6 I consider the years following the defeat of the ERA in 1982 to the election of President Bill Clinton in 1992. Many observers of NOW note that this period marks its transition from a social movement organization to an interest group. At the same time, NOW's strategies remained remarkably consonant with its governance structure. NOW leaders had largely failed in their earlier attempts to shift the group's activity toward the electoral arena, but they proved more successful in this regard after 1982. Nevertheless, this victory involved constraints and concessions. The process of moving toward electoral activism in NOW after the ERA's demise in 1982 illustrates how grassroots activists, with the aid of NOW's governance structure, limited leaders' ability to commit fully to a new strategy. In chapter 7 I show how NOW's strategic choices since the 1992 elections continue to mark it as a "radical" or vanguard organization, at least as compared with every other mainstream feminist group. In chapter 8 I conclude by considering the effects of NOW's governance structure on its strategic development and the consequences for its future growth and vitality. Notwithstanding NOW's success at survival and its enhancement of political engagement among its members, its governance structure (and the policies that are pursued as a result of it) diminishes NOW's ability to appeal to wider publics. This analysis does not suggest that the National Organization for Women is inherently inadequate in some sense but rather illustrates an irony: the most representative and participatory voluntary associations may also be among the least politically powerful and the least well equipped to increase civic engagement or political participation more generally.

2. Inventing NOW

Principles and Processes, 1966–1971

We were talking about a *revolution*.

Betty Friedan

Do foundings "imprint" a structural form on organizations? Arthur L. Stinchcombe makes this suggestion, and it is a useful way to think about NOW.[1] Officially, the inception of the National Organization for Women took place in 1966 during the annual national conference of the State Commissions on the Status of Women. The initial formation of an organization does not complete its founding, however. That task is finished when a group firmly establishes the set of guiding principles and formal decision-making procedures that together constitute its governance structure, a process NOW did not complete until 1971.

Conventional wisdom about the founding of the National Organization for Women tells this story: a group of middle-class white women formed NOW for the purpose of elevating the legal status and improving the employment prospects of women like themselves. The historical record undermines this reductive yet widespread characterization. NOW's founding group of members undoubtedly overrepresented middle-class women since they initially organized at a government-sponsored meeting of the State Status of Women Commissions, to which only well-known advocates of

women's issues were invited. Many other advocacy organizations, however, could be (and were) chastised for their middle-
class base. In 1966, for example, the African American congressman Adam Clayton Powell (D-N.Y.) urged women at a meeting of
the National Association of Colored Women's Clubs to "shake off
the mink coat mentality that has alienated some from the black
masses."[2]

Though NOW founders and early activists shared similar educational and occupational backgrounds, they proved more diverse in
other ways. The Episcopal minister Dr. Pauli Murray and Equal Employment Opportunity (EEOC) commissioner Aileen Hernandez,
first "chairman" of NOW's board and later NOW president,[3] were
among the African Americans joining the new organization. A significant proportion of founders were union leaders, religious leaders,
sociologists, journalists, attorneys, and media executives. Early activists' goals were also diverse. NOW's Statement of Purpose not
only discussed the problems of professional women but noted that
"about two-thirds of Negro women are in the lowest paid occupa-
tions" and that the EEOC needed to become active on behalf of
black women, who were victims of "double discrimination."[4]

Another misleading idea about NOW's inception is that the group
sought fundamentally conservative goals by employing routine, insti-
tutionally focused tactics to bring about legal changes in the status of
middle-class women. NOW's Statement of Purpose explicitly repudi-
ates this view. Moreover, NOW's governance structure ultimately
fostered even more radical goals and tactics.[5]

A dynamic process involving both leaders and members, the institutionalization of NOW's governance structure ultimately reflected
and incorporated their resources, political experiences, and ideas.
The earliest NOW members conceived their new organization
through the lens of their own direct experiences with other groups,
including women's divisions in unions such as the United Auto
Workers (UAW), civil rights groups such as the National Association
for the Advancement of Colored People (NAACP), socialist organizations such as the Students for a Democratic Society (SDS), and

governmental bodies such as the Equal Employment Opportunity Commission, the Women's Bureau, and the various commissions on the status of women.

Shortly after its inception, NOW attracted many "new" activists who had been disaffected by their inability to capture the attention of their leaders in organizations such as the Student Nonviolent Coordinating Committee (SNCC), led by John Lewis, and the Congress of Racial Equality (CORE), led by James Farmer. Participation in other organizations by NOW founders and other early activists directly influenced the form that NOW's own principles, bureaucratic structure, and strategic choices would take.[6]

Setting the Stage: Resources and Political Opportunities

No social movement organization arises sui generis. The structure of political opportunities and the resources available to NOW in 1966 dramatically affected not only its creation but also its future trajectory. In 1960, for example, both political parties endorsed equal pay laws in their platforms.[7] Both parties and their presidential nominees that year took note of the fact that women were expected to vote in larger numbers than men in coming years. As a result, the parties intended to focus on attracting women voters and providing them with resources to bring others into the polling booths as well.[8]

Margaret Chase Smith's announcement of the launch of her presidential campaign in 1964; the activities of other civil rights organizations; the passage of new federal laws such as the Equal Pay Act in 1963 and the Civil Rights Act in 1964; the creation by the president of a federal commission to investigate women's legal, political, and social status; and finally the presence of mobilizable networks of experienced women's rights advocates all contributed to NOW's formation and earliest goals and tactics.

In NOW's 1966 "Invitation to Join," the group's founders asserted that the political environment was conducive for establishing a new women's rights organization. The "Invitation" noted that the group's formation was just one element of a "world-wide revolution of human rights now taking place within and beyond our borders":

> With so many Americans consciously concerned with full participa-
> tion of all our citizens, and with dramatic progress at many levels in
> recent years, the time is ripe for concerted, directed national action.
> The [1963] report of the President's Commission on the Status of
> Women, "American Women," has laid out a broad field of action. . . .
> The Civil Rights Act of 1964 prohibits discrimination in employment
> on the ground of sex, as well as of race, religion or national origin,
> and the Alabama jury case of 1966, *White vs. Crook*, brings women
> under the "equal protection of the law" as provided in the 5th and
> 14th amendments of the Constitution.[9]

Although initially conceived by a small group of individuals, NOW rapidly garnered an ideologically and experientially diverse membership, including women and men from labor unions, the business community, leftist activist organizations, and older groups such as the National Woman's Party. In 1967 NOW began coping with an influx of younger members who were attracted by the group's position on reproductive rights and by their own frustrations with other leftist civil rights and student groups that refused to address issues of women's rights.[10] The values, practices, and strategies these younger members brought with them also left a lasting impression on NOW.

Movements

The civil rights, peace, and socialist movements provided substantial opportunities and resources for the mobilization on behalf of women's rights before 1966, as scholars of the second wave of the women's movement have documented.[11] Social movement activity, like that of the civil rights movement in the 1950s and 1960s, both builds on and fosters networks of people and organizations possessing strategically useful—and transferable—information and skills. The presence of movement groups can also prepare the groundwork for the development of or advances by other social movements. In addition to the resources they engender, social movements that raise the awareness of a community or a society about one form of institutionalized injustice, for example, can raise the consciousness of other oppressed groups about the systemic origins of their own disadvantage. Similarly, earlier movements may heighten the polity's willingness to accept new demands.

The heavy participation of activist women in many of the organizations associated with movements, including the NAACP, CORE, SNCC, SDS, Women's Strike for Peace (WSP), and Women's International League for Peace and Freedom (WILPF), laid the groundwork for their subsequent involvement in women's rights groups. Even where their official roles remained constrained by restrictive gender roles, these women nevertheless learned valuable lessons, including how to organize communities, develop goals, implement a wide variety of tactics, and work with political parties and governmental institutions.

The tactics of movement organizations in which women participated in the decade before NOW's creation proved extremely varied and a rich resource for subsequent organizations. Women who were deeply involved in the labor and civil rights movements were not necessarily content to be silent foot soldiers in their organizations. At the conference organizing the new Negro American Labor Council in 1960 in Detroit, for example, women conducted a "successful revolt"—literally leading to fisticuffs—"forcing the expansion of the organization's all-male executive board to include two women vice presidents."[12] The Women's Strike for Peace also famously used noninstitutional means of making its point, as exemplified by its "unladylike" bestowal of raspberries on members of the House Un-American Activities Committee at a meeting investigating the movement in December 1962.[13]

Many civil rights organizations attracted media attention in the early 1960s as they grappled with internal disagreements over goals and tactics. When leaders in New York proposed a boycott of schools, for example, long-time leader of the NAACP Roy Wilkins argued that although such a tactic might sometimes be necessary, it was a "drastic action."[14] During this period new civil rights groups were formed by activists who advocated fresh tactical approaches and new goals. One former leader of an NAACP chapter in Brooklyn who became chairman of the new Citywide Committee on Integrated Schools argued, "The people seem to be way out in front of some of the big organizations, and they are demanding that new techniques be used. It is symptomatic of the revolutionary times in which we live that many people are not finding an outlet for their pent-up emotions in the existing organizations. . . . If I could have done what I wanted to do as a leader of an established civil rights organization, I would have remained there. I would not have started my own."[15]

As a result of sentiments like these, the more established civil rights groups soon began cautiously supporting demonstrations and other more confrontational protest activities while disavowing "adventurism."[16] Daniel Bell noted in 1964 that "most Negro leaders now find it difficult to speak out against 'militancy.' "[17] That year a coalition of civil rights and church groups that included old-guard organizations such as the NAACP formed the Council of Federated Organizations (COFO) to support a Mississippi voter registration drive launched by the Student Nonviolent Coordinating Committee (SNCC). Leaders of CORE and SNCC "described the operation as a program to arouse the political consciousness of the Negroes and to forge the political instruments needed to break the power of the whites."[18]

In fact, despite their general resistance to employing tactics likely to involve violence or disruption, by the mid 1960s, even the most reluctant group leaders acknowledged the pressure to expand their tactical repertoire. The *New York Times* reported the following: "Forty-five national Negro leaders declared yesterday that their civil rights strategy for 1965 would emphasize voter registration and political action." In a statement the leaders explained the motivation for their new strategic direction: "The Civil Rights Act of 1964 and the Economic Opportunity Act make possible a new climate in which the first responsibility of civil rights groups is to consolidate the political consciousness of Negro Americans gained through the effective use of their vote in the 1964 Presidential campaign."[19] The range of activities mentioned here, ranging from the "drastic" to the more mainstream, provided an extraordinarily broad spectrum of examples for the second wave of the women's rights movement.

The Influence of the State

Beginning in the 1940s, federal agencies such as the Department of Labor sponsored conferences that brought hundreds of prominent women together to consider, for example, "women's increasingly important role in the economy of the nation."[20] At such a conference in 1948, "representatives of eighty-seven civic and women's organizations, and of forty-three labor organizations [and] seventeen state labor administrators and eight representatives of management" heard President Harry Truman state that he "endorsed" the fight for equal pay and other women's rights.[21]

Although she could not be called a radical protagonist for women's rights, the assistant secretary of labor, Esther Peterson, was a strong supporter of legislation such as the Equal Pay Act. In 1962 she complained, "I get so annoyed . . . when I still hear people say that women work for pin money. Are the 4,600,000 women who are the sole support of their families working for pin money? Are the 7,500,000 mothers whose husbands earn less than $3,000 a year working for pin money? Are the widowed, separated and single women who have no man to support them working for pin money? Our studies show that these women work for the same reasons that men do."[22] By 1966 one could order a booklet outlining, by state, "many of a wife's important rights," published by the Women's Bureau.[23]

Organizations such as the United Nations also kept issues of women's rights on the agenda between the end of the American suffrage movement and the beginning of the new feminist movement. The UN pioneered the concept of a Commission on the Status of Women in 1946, for example. In 1947 the UN conducted a worldwide survey of more than seventy-four countries on women's role and rights for its Commission on the Status of Women.[24] After years of discussion the UN General Assembly ratified a Convention on Political Rights for Women in 1952. (The United States did not sign the pact: "The Eisenhower Administration was interested in promoting equality for women but did not feel that this aim could be advanced by 'treaty coercion' ").[25] In 1953 the UN's Commission on the Legal Status of Women worked to formulate plans to "remove discriminations against women in such matters as family law and property rights."[26] Brooklyn congressman Emanuel Celler later began introducing bills in the House to establish a U.S. version of the various UN's women's commissions. Celler's stated intention was to avoid passing the Equal Rights Amendment, which, he argued, threatened to usurp states' rights and "destroy protective labor laws for women."[27] Celler realized this goal years after he first proposed it, in the form of John F. Kennedy's 1961 executive order creating the twenty-six-member President's Commission on the Status of Women (PCSW), chaired by Eleanor Roosevelt.[28]

One of this commission's early actions was an extensive study of the legal, political, social, and economic position of women. In a wide-ranging and strongly worded report in 1963, the commission documented the many areas in which women's status remained subordinate to men's. One of its recommendations was the creation of a more permanent organization to continue this research. Shortly thereafter Kennedy created the Citizens' Advisory Council on the Status of Women (CACSW) and a parallel, cabinet-level Interdepartmental Committee on the Status of Women (ICSW).

The U.S. Commissions on the Status of Women helped create and extend networks of mobilizable women with their own personal and political resources. Beginning in 1964 state-level commissions met together annually in Washington under the aegis of the ICSW, drawing 322 participants in 1965. The meetings and discussions at these state- and national-level conferences gathered together like-minded women; the reports they generated laid a framework for a women's rights platform and plan of attack. President Lyndon B. Johnson's announcement in 1965 of a conference to consider how to achieve the fair and effective administration of the 1964 Civil Rights Act provided yet another venue for women to gather in order to apply pressure for equal rights.[29]

Networks

Individuals concerned with women's rights also participated in and communicated through a broad network of well-established groups and clubs such as the National Federation of Business and Professional Women's Clubs (BPW), the League of Women Voters (LWV), the National Council of Negro Women, the National Woman's Party, the Junior League, the American Association of University Women (AAUW), women's divisions of Zionist groups, and even parent-teacher associations. Some members of these groups crossed paths through their participation in Commissions on the Status of Women, but others met at less formal local meetings. In 1956, for example, three hundred individuals from various women's clubs in the East gathered at an annual conference sponsored in part by the Connecticut-based Service Bureau for Women's Organizations.[30]

Women in associations that appeared nonpolitical took advantage of their information and connections to pursue governmental issues that concerned them. In 1959, for example, local chapters of the League of Women Voters, the Parent-Teacher Association Council, the University Women's Education Committee, and the National Association of College Women joined together to protest school funding cuts in Norwalk, Connecticut. Much to the chagrin of the mayor, who urged sanctions against the groups for acting politically, they responded in a joint letter: "You must surely be aware . . . that [we] are not the same as political parties, but, rather, are civic-minded groups whose members are of all political persuasions and concerned with the welfare of Norwalk. We consider it our responsibility as well as our right to present the facts in this matter to the community."[31]

Labor unions and professional associations such as the Women's National Press Club also provided critical networks for women's rights activists. Various women's, human rights, and civil rights divisions of the AFL-CIO and other labor associations included women in decision-making capacities and addressed women's equity in the workplace. In 1962 "more than 200 delegates to the American Newspaper Guild convention demanded in a resolution . . . that newspapers end employment discrimination against women and minority groups."[32]

In addition to participation in "nonpolitical" groups, women were heavily involved in political parties, yet another means of encountering like-minded potential activists.[33] For example, Emma Guffey Miller was a member of the Pennsylvania Democratic National Committee the same year (1960) in which she was also elected to the national chairmanship of the National Woman's Party.[34]

In the early 1960s educational institutions and foundations also brought women together by conducting and funding programs to encourage women to broaden their experiences. In 1960, for example, the Radcliffe Institute for Independent Study formed to help married women "resume and progress in their professional development." By 1966 "more than 500 women [participated] in research, in seminars, or [by] receiving vocational and educational guidance."[35] The Carnegie Foundation funded similar programs through the auspices of Barnard College from 1962 to 1966.[36]

Such networks had considerable density and range. In 1965 lawyer (later reverend) Dr. Pauli Murray addressed the National Council of Women of the United States, indicting the use of sex-segregated classified advertisements. Her speech prompted union activist and writer Betty Friedan to contact her. Later that year Murray, along with feminist and Department of Justice lawyer Mary O. Eastwood, published an analysis of judicial discrimination against women in the *George Washington Law Review*; "Jane Crow and the Law," which examined the effect of Title VII on women's rights.[37]

By the time Betty Friedan met Murray, she had already been attracting significant attention from the media. A freelance writer who often covered women and labor issues, Friedan published *The Feminine Mystique* in 1963, documenting how cultural and demographic events since the depression allowed women to consider and experience a wider range of personal choices in work and family life than ever before. At the same time, she observed, the sociopolitical climate of the 1950s and early 1960s fostered the idea that women's nature achieved its highest expression in the arena of home and family. Women who rejected or resisted their "natural" sphere risked being seen as emotionally or psychologically unbalanced. Parents encouraged their children to marry early, cutting young women off from expanded opportunities.[38] Friedan's well-received work provided her with opportunities to speak around the country on women's issues. Her celebrity attracted the attention of feminists involved in Washington politics, the State Status of Women Commissions, and the National Woman's Party as well as those concerned with enforcing Title VII of the 1964 Civil Rights Act.

NOW's Inception

The origin of the National Organization for Women is largely attributable to the growing conviction, held by an "underground" (to use Friedan's term) network of feminist and women's rights sympathizers, of the need for an entirely new organization dedicated to pressing for women's issues. The underground network included activists who remembered the first wave of the feminist movement in addition to institutional insiders such as Richard Graham and lawyer Sunny Pressman, both employed at the EEOC. According to Friedan, these men and women recruited and cajoled her to consider forming a new women's group.[39] She wrote:

> My phone began to ring in the middle of the night with calls from suffragettes, dauntless old women now in their eighties and nineties who had chained themselves to the White House fence to get the vote. These leftover feminists who refused to die were seen as a joke and a nuisance by Washington political observers, even by the underground concerned with jobs and Title VII. But now these ancient fighters were calling me and saying in their wavery voices: "You've got to do something about getting Title VII enforced."[40]

The underground pressured Friedan to hold a press conference at the 1966 annual meeting of the State Commissions on the Status of Women to publicize the lack of vigor with which the EEOC pursued Title VII complaints. Friedan initially resisted both the idea of a press conference and the suggestion that she form an "NAACP for women." Since she was not a member of any commission, she used a press pass to attend the fateful 1966 meeting. Friedan agreed, at the behest of Pauli Murray and labor activist Dorothy Haener, to host a gathering in her hotel room of a small group of conference participants who shared a frustration with the lack of progress on women's issues.

At the meeting Friedan's companions-in-arms decided to give the national commission another opportunity to show its commitment to the full enforcement of Title VII and to action versus rhetoric. After spending the evening discussing the EEOC's inattention to employment discrimination against women and possible remedies, attendees at Friedan's meeting planned to present a resolution to the conference that "demand[ed] enforcement of Title VII and call[ed] for Richard Graham's reappointment. Graham was the only one of the four male EEOC commissioners who was sympathetic to women's claims and his term was nearly up."[41] The next day, however, Esther Peterson, executive vice chairman of the commission and assistant secretary of labor, rebuffed their efforts, telling the dissident faction that "the purpose of the conference was to share information, not to take action, and that no resolutions would be allowed."[42]

Spurred by this failure to influence the commission's activities, the discontented conference participants sketched the purpose and outline of a new organization they dubbed the National Organization for Women, planning an organizing conference for four months later. Above all, the founders wanted their group to "be free to act . . . and be free to speak out unhampered by official connection with the government."[43] Founders and charter members included Marguerite Rawalt, a government lawyer; Caruthers Berger, a government lawyer and activist in the National Woman's Party; and members of the UAW women's bureau, including Dorothy Haener.

For many years after NOW's inception, the group depended on the expertise of this first cohort of members. As members of government bodies, labor organizers, political party activists, members of the National Association of Women Lawyers (NAWL) and the National Federation of Business and Professional Women's Clubs—the most valuable resources that organizers brought to the newly formed group included their professional networks and their knowledge of politics and of the media. At least thirty of NOW's earliest members were attorneys or judges, for example, and many of the group's first initiatives took advantage of their legal skills.[44] Even NOW's office space depended on members' occupational status: the group found its first home at the University of Wisconsin and its second at the United Auto Workers' office.[45]

Guiding Principles

"The ideology of those of us who started the women's rights movement was not sexual or political," Friedan recalls. "I would have said, then, we had no ideology. It was simply the idea of equality, of American democracy."[46] Nevertheless, NOW's leaders and members codified the principles that mattered most to them in formal documents in ways that are apparent almost four decades later.

The interpretation of NOW's principles grew more expansive under the influence of members and leaders of the "younger and more radical" branch of the women's movement, although the essential elements of NOW's principles are visible in the group's earliest founding documents. By 1971 the National Organization for Women's guiding principles incorporated a commitment to remaining on the vanguard of the women's movement, to being an activist rather than an educational group, to maintaining political independence from governmental institutions, to focusing on a diverse set of issues and tactics, and to encouraging grassroots participation. The second component of NOW's governance structure, the group's formal decision-making processes, in turn offered members significant opportunities for representation and participation. These opportunities reinforced NOW's adherence to these principles over time. NOW's guiding principles reflected the past political experiences of both the founding members and those who joined the group over the next several years. Some activists had defected from other social movement groups when they discovered, for example, that the groups they were devoting their energies to, including SNCC and the

Black Panthers, refused to acknowledge women's oppression. In response to dismissive attitudes, women's liberation activists formed groups including the Feminists, New York Radical Women, the Chicago Women's Liberation Union, the Furies and the Women's International Terrorist Conspiracy from Hell (WITCH). These organizations eschewed hierarchical structures and elitism. They operated so that the broadest number of women would benefit from the opportunity to learn and participate in all aspects of the organization's activities: leadership opportunities should be open to all women, for example.[47]

The vision that radical women's liberation activists constructed of an ideal feminist organizational form soon became incorporated into NOW's own guiding principles, which, by the end of NOW's founding in 1971, included what Wini Breines calls "prefigurative" elements. Breines describes the prefigurative politics practiced by the New Left:

> The term . . . is used to designate an essentially anti-organizational politics characteristic of the movement, as well as parts of the New Left leadership, and may be recognized in counter-institutions, demonstrations and the attempt to embody personal and anti-hierarchical values in politics. Participatory democracy was central to prefigurative politics. . . . The crux of prefigurative politics imposed substantial tasks, the central one being to create and sustain within the live practice of the movement, relationships and political forms that "prefigured" and embodied the desired society.[48]

A Vanguard Feminist Organization　One of NOW's earliest documents, its Statement of Purpose, represents NOW's conviction that the improvement of women's status hinged on their representation in the halls of Congress, in party leadership, and in the judiciary, academia, and industry. NOW founders wanted to take action to become "part of the decision-making mainstream of American political, economic and social life."[49] For these feminists, at this moment in history, joining the "mainstream" was a radical notion.

The demand to become a part of the decision-making mainstream seems consistent with a politically moderate organization uninterested in addressing the root causes of women's oppression. It also seems to indicate a narrow, middle-class conception of equality. Yet the Statement of Purpose documents NOW leaders' awareness of the economic inequalities facing African American and other women occupying the lowest rung of the employment ladder as well as the obstacles women encountered in seeking higher education.

NOW's founders were prepared to form a "revolutionary" organization well before the influence of the "radical" women's liberation movement several years later. The Statement repeatedly describes the limitations placed on women's advancement by bedrock social institutions such as marriage and motherhood. NOW founders did not shy away from acknowledging the fundamental changes that would be required in the social structure to bring about an egalitarian culture: "We reject the current assumptions that a man must carry the sole burden of supporting himself, his wife, and family, and that a woman is automatically entitled to lifelong support by a man upon her marriage. . . . In the interests of human dignity of women, we will protest, and endeavor to change, the false image of women so prevalent in the mass media and in the texts, ceremonies, laws, and practices of our major social institutions."[50]

In fact, one reason Friedan felt so reluctant initially to organize a women's organization was that she did not see the NAACP model—the one frequently suggested to her—as radical enough for the purpose. She noted, "The NAACP analogy never seemed quite right, even at the time. We were talking about a *revolution*, and though the NAACP fought for black people (not like those women's organizations so afraid of being called 'feminist'), the NAACP was not considered a radical organization at all."[51] In fact, despite the increasing demands from civil rights activists for a more forceful strategic plan and the apparent support of American "opinion leaders" for "direct-action demonstrations," the *New York Times* reported, "It is clear that the men who in the past turned to the courts and negotiating table are prepared to continue on this course, shunning violence and unnecessary gestures."[52]

The commitment of NOW leaders to maintaining the group's vanguard status together with their insistence on forging connections with the wider activist political community allowed the values and tactics of the New Left and of women's liberation activists to permeate NOW's principles, practices, and strategies. The energy of and attention on the women's liberation movement provided competition for NOW, spurring its leaders to jockey to maintain the group's status as the leading women's rights organization in the country. Acknowledging the impact of these newer organizations, NOW member and reporter for *Newsday* Dolores Alexander argued that "if we in NOW are to stay in the vanguard of this revolution, we are faced with the responsibility of developing an ideology for the future. Our task is to venture beyond that 'primitive' stage, break new ground, formulate unprecedented policy: visionary, undogmatic and, above all, responsible."[53]

Activism Not Education   Experience with the Women's Bureau, other women's organizations, and the various Commissions on the Status of Women impressed on the NOW founders the fact that studies and reports did little to improve women's sociopolitical status. In its 1966 "Invitation to Join" the founders proclaimed that NOW is a "new national organization formed to take action to bring women into full participation in the mainstream of American society NOW. . . . It will not generally engage in independent research but will act on the basis of information and recommendations available from status of women commissions, government agencies and specialized organizations."[54]

The Statement of Purpose pointed out that the commissions' "excellent reports have not been fully implemented. Such Commissions have power only to advise. They have no power to enforce their recommendations; nor have they the freedom to organize American women and men and press for action on them."[55] In contrast to existing models of women's organizational behavior, "we organize to initiate or support action . . . the time has come to move beyond the abstract argument, discussion and symposia over the status and special nature of women which has raged in America in recent years; the time has come to confront, with concrete action, the conditions that now prevent women from enjoying the equality of opportunity and freedom which is their right, as individual Americans, and as human beings."[56]

First president Betty Friedan continually urged action on NOW members and leaders. In a January 1968 report she cajoled NOW members: "Dedicated as we are to action and not just words in NOW . . . now it is up to every member and chapter . . . to act to bring our Bill of Rights for Women in 1968 to the attention of local political representatives and candidates as well as to your representatives in Washington, and to devise new ways of exposing and combating sex discrimination."[57]

Political Independence NOW's Statement of Purpose asserts, "NOW will hold itself independent of any political party in order to mobilize the political power of all women and men intent on our goals." Citizen groups often express the need to form organizations that remain independent of both governmental bodies and political parties. The intransigent opposition of the Department of Labor's Women's Bureau to the Equal Rights Amendment, for example, led the National Woman's Party to complain that the bureau considered itself "all-powerful, directing the actions of government agencies, senators, and representatives on the ERA issue." The party called for the bureau's dissolution several times.[58] (The Woman's Bureau reversed its opposition in 1970.) Similarly, when the Negro American Labor Council formed in 1960 (headed by A. Phillip Randolph, vice president of the American Federation of Labor and Congress of Industrial Organizations), for example, its constitution specifically prohibited "political activities by local or state affiliates . . . in line with the group's intention to function on a nonpartisan basis and to shun the basic alliance with the Democratic party that characterized the political policy of most [AFL] units."[59]

Feminists' dismal record of success with the tactic of cooperating with political entities, including the Women's Bureau, the women's divisions of the political parties, the Equal Employment Opportunity Commission, and the Commissions on the Status of Women, convinced them that NOW must follow a different path. In an early interview one of the five men on NOW's board, Reverend Dean Lewis, was asked why the organization felt the need to become active in the political arena. "Politics?" he responded, "What do you have for women in that field? Women's political auxiliaries. They are put aside in nice separate structures without policy-making powers."[60] Cofounder Alice Rossi reiterated the fact that NOW was created because of the "conviction that there is a pressing need for an independent organization, free of involvement with political organization on the state and federal level, which can move quickly to apply pressure when and where it is needed."[61]

Women's liberation groups, which promoted a grassroots empowerment and anti-elitist ethic that ultimately infiltrated NOW through cross-cutting group memberships, also raised the issue of the potential for social movement organizations to be co-opted by established political institutions such as political parties. Movements that cooperated too closely with government institutions or participated too heavily in mainstream forms of politics risked circumscribing their values and goals in order to maintain their credibility in those spheres. For example, as a result of their close identification with the Democratic Party, major civil rights groups called on their members and the leaders and members of other rights groups to curtail their protest activity until after the 1964 presidential elections.[62]

Diverse Tactics and Issues   Before the 1960s, according to Leila Rupp and Verta Taylor, "feminists were willing to use almost any strategy . . . to further their goals as long as it did not involve engaging in mass protest and other disruptive tactics." At the time of NOW's inception such reluctance had begun to fade.[63] In its "Invitation to Join," NOW founders argued that "as a private, voluntary, self-selected group it will establish its own procedures and not be limited in its targets for action or methods of operation by official protocol." By 1966 NOW founders, along with the rest of the country, were quite familiar with the extraordinarily rich array of tactics employed by the labor, civil rights, and peace movements in the previous decade. Their tactics ranged from the pursuit of carefully selected court cases, to rent strikes, sit-ins, freedom rides, voter registration drives, the creation of the Mississippi Freedom Democratic Party, and even a violent demonstration at UN headquarters in New York.

Between the 1940s and the 1960s, women may have felt they had, as Rupp and Taylor note, "little choice but to adopt legal change and institutionalized reform as [their] ultimate goals, and to use strategies that were respectable and non-disruptive."[64] Having witnessed the diversity of tactics employed by other rights groups in the years before NOW's inception, its founders intended to follow suit. The radical women's liberation groups that organized several years later routinized the use of extra-institutional means of achieving social and political change. Their example encouraged NOW's strategic evolution with the use of techniques such as consciousness-raising and with the incorporation of ever more vanguard issues, including those concerning sexual freedom and lesbian rights.

Grassroots Participation

NOW's Statement of Purpose emphasized the need for women to become true partners in governing in order to redress inequities, repeatedly asserting that women must be recruited and mobilized to secure their own rights. NOW exhorted women to take charge of their social, political, and economic lives:

> We believe that women will do most to create a new image of women by *acting* now, and by speaking out in behalf of their *own* equality, freedom and human dignity—not in pleas for special privilege, nor in enmity toward men, who are also victims of the current, half-equality between the sexes—but in an *active*, self-respecting partnership with men. By so doing, women will develop confidence in their *own* ability to determine *actively*, in partnership with men, the conditions of their life, their choices, their future and their society.[65] (Emphases added.)

Two influential founders, sociologist Alice Rossi and Kathryn Clarenbach, pushed Friedan to reaffirm her commitment to involving as many women as possible in the new group. Rossi wrote:

I certainly agree with you on the need for an independent organization dedicated to pressing hard and quickly on topics that are of direct concern to women and to the relations between men and women. I do not think, however, that such an organization should be a tiny group of elite persons, since there are so many situations in American society in which what will be politically and socially effective is not just direct personal influence, or quotes from prominent women, but the pressure represented by numerical strength.[66]

Friedan reassured Rossi: "My stress against a 'big bureaucratic organization' did not mean I want a small select group, but rather an organization directed to action and not to perpetuating its own bureaucracy in the fashion of most women's organizations, all of which it would seem to me to be completely ineffective, and none of which even dare to tackle the problems we want to tackle."[67]

NOW members connected with the radical women's liberation movement worked to further cement a membership-focused, participatory ethos in NOW's guiding principles.[68] As Jo Freeman notes, "Empowerment of women is one of the few ideas on which feminists have agreed virtually from the beginning."[69]

Decision-Making Processes: Structuring Representation and Participation

The establishment of NOW's organizational routines and guiding principles took years. During this time leaders sought solutions to NOW's persistent monetary, bureaucratic and philosophic challenges by formalizing the organization's structure and by clarifying members' role in group decision making. At the same time, NOW members new and old pushed the group to broaden its interpretation of its mission and, as a result, its principles.

Formalizing Member Representation in Elections and Policymaking To Friedan's chagrin, the process of constructing a decision-making structure occupied an extraordinary amount of the group's time. NOW's proposed bylaws emphasized the importance of members' influence, stipulating, for example, that an annual membership conference would determine NOW's governing policy. The bylaws also provided for term-limited board members, an Executive Committee, and a president. Members attending the 1966 organizing conference amended the proposed bylaws in significant ways, increasing the number of board members, providing for membership election of national officers and board members, and otherwise ensuring that the national conference reflect members' interests.[70] They also created task forces where members would be empowered to develop the organization's philosophy, targets for action, and strategies.[71]

A major area of ongoing debate centered on balancing the founders' desire to maintain NOW's action-oriented focus with members' concern with fostering intraorganizational discussion and solidifying their formal representation in the group. Reporting on the matter in 1969, Friedan noted:

> This will be . . . our third try at a Constitution to mesh NOW's specific needs and the democratic will of its members. Previously, the Steering Committee and the National Organizing Conference were not able to agree on draft constitutions modeled after other organizations such as the American Veterans Committee, the American Civil Liberties Union, and national labor unions, nor did we want to model ourselves after women's organizations whose constitutions preclude the action to which we are dedicated.[72]

In part the continuing debate over NOW's decision-making processes reflected the influence of the women's liberation movement. Although NOW's initial set of decision-making procedures provided for a significant amount of representation and participation of members, individuals involved in both NOW and the newer "radical" women's groups pressured NOW's national leadership to become even more grassroots oriented. An important NOW member and leader of the New York Chapter in 1968, Ti-Grace Atkinson, broke from NOW to form a new organization ultimately called The Feminists. The schism occurred when Atkinson, formerly a strong ally of Friedan, came to "view the power relationship between NOW's executive board and the general membership as a copycat extension of the standard forms of male domination." She argued that in the place of the board, NOW should eliminate executive offices and establish "rotating chairmen chosen by lot from the general membership." The members of Atkinson's chapter rebuffed her reforms, however, and she resigned.[73]

Friedan emphasized the nature of the distribution of power and the structure of accountability in NOW. Ultimate power over policy choices would reside with the members, who were also empowered to elect NOW's leaders:

> The structure we have now agreed upon . . . gives the basic power to the membership as a whole [and has] provisions to prevent domination by any one group or region, to provide representation for those unable to attend, and to insure continuity. Between such conferences, the national board of 35, including the five national officers, will be free to act, meeting every three months. Between its meetings, the five officers will be free to execute agreed policy.[74]

Elections would be as representative of the membership as possible while allowing elected officers the freedom to conduct the business of the group between conferences.

Friedan expressed some hesitation over the shifts in NOW's decision-making apparatus that fostered such a high degree of membership power. Although some changes augured well for the group, such as the creation of a new regional arrangement that would rationalize NOW's structure, Friedan worried that the more radical members of the organization would take advantage of the many opportunities to shape NOW's politics to the detriment of the group: "There is a need for discussion and writing on the ideological thrust of NOW. To continue to stay in the vanguard of the women's liberation movement NOW must continue to emphasize that man is not the enemy but is the fellow victim of discrimination; we must work for radical changes in society, but meanwhile, push for child care centers and other devices which enable women to progress here and now."[75] Other NOW leaders, however, expressed optimism that NOW's bureaucracy would enhance NOW's stability while allowing it to adapt as the women's movement evolved. In July 1970 Chairman Wilma Scott Heide wrote of the changes: "NOW has been and is the catalyst of this emerging, most profound social change the world has yet known. . . . [With the organization's leadership and structural change] we can hope to move to a sounder financial and organizational foundation without becoming institutionalized."[76]

Incorporating and Engaging Members and Chapters

Establishing an acceptable system of representation proved to be one of many issues urgently requiring the attention of NOW leaders. Despite its rapid rise to national attention, NOW struggled for many years with the practical realities of fully incorporating and engaging its members. National NOW strained to compile up-to-date information about its membership and chapters, to maintain accurate accounts of donors and activists, to answer pleas for help from the public and its own members, to establish internal lines of communication, and to impose the national structure on independent chapters. The group also battled to stay financially solvent.

Initially, NOW founders did not clearly spell out the role of chapters in the organization: "It was agreed that NOW will basically function as a national organization of individual members, with provisions, however, for setting up local chapters where desired."[77] Chapters became formally incorporated into NOW bylaws at a February 1967 national board meeting. Chapters quickly formed in major cities such as New York and Chicago, but by 1970 only ten officially recognized chapters existed—despite the fact that the group's membership rolls rose to three thousand that year.[78] Freeman observes that "local chapters have sprung up almost incidentally, usually through the efforts of local people, not national organizers."[79]

New chapters lacked well-defined bridges to the national organization:

The national newsletter came out only quarterly, and occasionally not at all. Letters to the national office often were not referred to the right official or even answered. Requests for material were backlogged for months and occasionally lost. Chapter presidents did not get the National Task Force Reports and thus were often unable to connect local task force projects with national efforts. . . . Potential members could not find the local chapter and were not referred by the national office. Other people wanted to start NOW chapters, but could not find out how to.[80]

NOW made slow progress on details such as membership recruitment. Rossi noted that at the October 1966 organizing conference "it seemed to me a high priority matter was membership recruitment. But no serious discussion of this took place."[81] At an "informal" meeting of thirty-five members (including six board members) in January 1967, a consensus felt that "with respect to the entire area of recruiting, questions were raised about getting application forms and membership acknowledgements more readily from [NOW headquarters in] Detroit. It was feared that momentum and enthusiasm are being lost where there is a delay."[82]

One meeting attendee, Chairman Kathryn Clarenbach, seized the opportunity to outline the weaknesses and strengths of the organization. Several NOW leaders insisted on considering as many opinions as possible in routine decision making, she argued, yet key questions concerning the group's vision and tactical choices remained unresolved.[83] She emphasized that scarce financial resources as well as the broad geographic dispersal of leaders and members hampered the organization. Few funds existed to reimburse board or committee members, let alone the membership, for attendance at national conferences or board meetings. In addition, serious deterrents to participation undermined NOW's ability to fully engage all members and chapters in shaping the group's actions and positions.

The incapacity of the national office to fully inform and incorporate its members into its operations meant that more than a year after its inception, NOW's founders and board members retained the greatest influence on conceiving and initiating actions and setting issue priorities. Since few specific channels existed to accept the input of rank-and-file members, leaders' and board members' initiatives and positions did not necessarily represent broad constituencies within NOW. Thus President Friedan and other executive leaders had significant leeway to act independently of the board and the membership. Whereas some founders approved of Friedan's penchant for rapid and independent decision making, her quick commitment of NOW to some controversial positions left others distinctly uncomfortable.

In her detailed memo to the board in June 1967, Clarenbach suggested, "Local chapters (and state) may turn out to be the major action vehicles as well as the route to membership involvement. They must have a part in formulation of task force statements."[84] In this memo Clarenbach laid out the main organizational issues that still needed major attention a year after NOW's founding; a persistent theme is her sense that pathways must be created to facilitate members' input into NOW's agenda and structure. Clarenbach worried that "priority for action items needs thorough and constant reevaluation. The 'crisis' approach to action does not allow for initiative on our part with proper preparation, or for the fullest understanding and participation of members." As a result, Clarenbach urged the "systematic representation" of the membership by officers and board members and by the members of committees, and suggested how chapters might be provided representation by delegates at the national conference.

Although members were due to evaluate NOW's "Task force statements" (the basis of NOW's action agenda and issue philosophy) at the 1967 national conference, it remained unclear how a broader range of members could participate in the formulation of these statements in the first place.

The composition of task forces needs to be drawn from total membership, yet geography and mobility are problems. . . . Task force statements are basic documents of philosophy and will only reflect total NOW thinking when they become the products of many minds. At the moment we only have the tentative, summary thoughts of one or two people, except for the Employment Statement, which was the work of 30 people, and even this should not be regarded as a final document.

Financial limitations hindered NOW's ability to solicit more input from activists. The group commanded few funds with which to purchase such basic necessities as postage, telephone lines, transportation, or even photocopies. During its first three years the organization's entire budget relied solely on member dues.[85] More than two years after its founding, NOW's national board was still required to authorize the "purchase [of] a locked file cabinet and necessary office supplies (i.e., duplicating supplies, stationery, postage, etc.) up to the amount of $200.00."[86] Although NOW leaders and board members recognized the need for a paid executive officer as 1968 drew to a close, this option seemed financially impossible. In November the board "made an urgent call to chapters to raise funds for the conduct of the national organization—the funds raised to be divided between the national and local treasuries on a 50–50 basis."[87] At this point NOW had virtually no funds at its disposal; the board viewed its plea as a "do-or-die effort."

Five months later the national board noted that the appeal had failed to remedy the group's urgent financial problems and reiterated the call for chapters to contribute. NOW's March 1969 newsletter emphasized that the funds were necessary because "we have grown too big too fast, and we can no longer exist on volunteer help alone. For lack of an office and staff, we have been only able to answer correspondence of immediate urgency. Communication with the chapters and individual members has been minimal; we have been unable to provide them with many services."[88] In February 1969 the group's available funds dropped to $600. By November 31, 1969, NOW's treasury held $1,735, and the group boasted approximately fifteen hundred active members.[89] At a December meeting the board approved a resolution that everyone present at the meeting "be asked to pledge [$]100 or 10 a month" to the group.[90] The national office reminded activists of the great expenses incurred in fighting court battles and maintaining and improving communication with the membership:

Any organization needs three things in order to be effective: meaning, members, and money. We have the first two but very little of the third.

Up until now a major problem has been just making our existence known. Recently publicity in the mass media about our organization and about the plight of women has helped. But the publicity has carried with it two dangers; people think that we are bigger than we are, and they assume that mass recognition of the woman problem means that it's solved. . . . But understand that the real struggle, the work stage, is still very much with us.[91]

Despite this paucity of resources, NOW leaders continued to work to involve its chapters and members in the group's decision-making processes. In May 1968, for example, the organization began producing a newsletter called *NOW ACTS* in order to publish board decisions and conference resolutions and report on chapters' activities. Soon thereafter NOW national also decided to hire one staff member, though at the cost of closing its headquarters. "Operating on the slimmest budget, Miss [Dolores] Alexander literally has taken NOW into her home. The national office in Washington DC was closed in order to save money; and the files, mimeo machine, et al. were moved temporarily into her 2 room apartment."[92]

To further mitigate the group's most serious structural, bureaucratic, and financial weaknesses, NOW board members proposed reforms in December 1969. They decided to publish the national newsletter more frequently, to fund it with advertising revenues, and to propose restructuring the organization along regional lines to facilitate communication between members and national leaders. Regionalization would also distribute some of the daily organizing tasks, too much of which rested on the shoulders of the national office. For the same reason, the board also proposed expanding the number of national vice presidents, giving each a specific task. NOW's leaders explained the changes in the winter 1970 newsletter:

NOW's tremendous growth has created its own problems in communication, in feelings of isolation, and in the too heavy or concentrated leadership load. The board, in meetings in San Francisco and New Orleans, envisioned a new NOW structure that would minimize the responsibilities of any one individual *and simultaneously allow all members and geographic areas more participation.* The effect of the amendments on the bylaws . . . is to reorganize NOW on a regional basis.[93] (emphasis added)

Among the tasks redistributed to regional entities were fund-raising and the mailing of information from the national office to board members and chapters.[94] Four regional directors represented the South, East, Midwest, and West.[95] The directors, together with four new vice presidents (responsible for fundraising, public relations, legal activities, and legislative tasks) as well as the president and chairman of the board, formed an executive committee.

By the close of 1971 NOW claimed four to five thousand members and one hundred fifty chapters. Together NOW leaders and activists had succeeded in building a framework for the group's decision-making processes and principles. NOW's guiding principles, established by the end of 1971, reflected both founders' and newer members' convictions about the need for their group to be an active, independent, vanguard force for women's rights. The principles also spelled out NOW's commitment to mobilizing men and women for its cause.

In addition to forging a framework of values, by the end of NOW's founding period the group had reformed its structure and procedures, spreading responsibility for tasks and leadership among regions and chapters. NOW's decision-making processes emphasized the financial, administrative, and substantive participation of members.

3. NOW's Strategic Evolution

> We in NOW must realize that the black struggle has
> accomplished no real revolution. . . . We are at a
> point of departure from it and all others.
>
> NOW ACTS

Although NOW formed task forces in 1966 to research and report on
the areas of education, employment, legal and political rights, family
life (social innovation), poverty, mass media image, NOW membership, and finances, coordinated implementation of the resulting recommendations took time. Throughout NOW's early years discussions
concerning goals and priorities frequently yielded to the exigencies of
creating a formal structure for the group and to keeping it viable. But
in 1967, President Friedan expressed relief that that month's board
meeting was the "most successful and productive . . . to date, since
we were able to spend a good part of it, for the first time, on substantive issues instead of structure and housekeeping details."[1]

Goals

Leaders and members at NOW's October 1966 organizing conference agreed on further "targets for action," which included (1) equal
opportunity for women in employment, (2) educational opportunities for women, (3) fundamental social equality between sexes, (4)

changing the stereotypical images of women, (5) addressing the problem of women in poverty, and (6) gaining equal rights and responsibilities for women as citizens. Within six months the board held two press conferences announcing the group's existence and purpose, one in November 1966 in New York City and another in Washington, D.C., in January 1967.[2]

Although, as we have seen, coordinated activity with members and chapters was complicated by financial and other limitations, national NOW managed to engage a number of political issues fairly quickly. To pursue its targets, NOW sent letters to the EEOC and met with EEOC officials, took a position supporting women in the military, pressured President Johnson to increase his appointment of women to federal positions, and filed a legal brief in support of a flight attendant's employment dispute.

NOW's early structural and organizational deficits gave its first officers a great deal of freedom to make decisions without consulting other board members. In a letter to Clarenbach, chairman of NOW's Temporary Steering Committee, Rossi protested, asserting that NOW's highest priority should be focusing on consensus issues in order to build membership and solidarity. As a mass membership group, NOW should concentrate on its image in order to attract new adherents. "Can't you just see the field day the press would have on 'American women urged to join our boys in Vietnam jungles'?"[3] She argued that NOW should remain focused on women's issues and not on what she viewed as nonpolitical debates: "Managing women's issues is a big enough job and to move into more peripheral issues should only be done, I should think, after we have a viable organization and have laid down some guidelines for executive officers to follow in pursuit of our general goals."[4] In December 1966 Rossi expanded on her objections: "I am very distressed about the premature actions taken. There seems to be absolutely no reason for seeking 'presidential appointments' at this juncture, before we are fully organized in details, and have so small a membership list. There is much 'in-house education' to do in our own group, and a lot of specific targets to work on while we build a reputation and a membership that amounts to something."[5]

Despite such reservations, other NOW leaders immediately began working to make the new organization's political presence felt. In fact, Friedan insisted that conducting meetings with officials and with potential allies,

> need not wait upon the completion and adoption of a constitution which will give us the formal structure for setting up chapters. The many hundreds of men and women who have joined NOW as the result of the public word of NOW's goals since early November are very eager indeed to contribute personal efforts and energies to concrete projects. Our Statement of Purpose and the decisions already made by the Executive Committee on concrete objectives to which we have begun to address ourselves nationally provide ample framework for local and state action.[6]

Members soon had another opportunity to weigh in on the goals and tactics they wanted NOW to pursue. In 1967 members at the national conference drafted a "Bill of Rights for Women," intended to embody the goals set out in NOW's Statement of Purpose. As adopted, the Bill of Rights demanded the enforcement of equal employment opportunity laws, maternity leave rights and Social Security benefits for stay-at-home mothers, the federal provision of child day-care centers, a guarantee of equal and unsegregated education, equal job training opportunities, and allowances for women in poverty.

With Friedan's support, NOW's members also voted to support the Equal Rights Amendment and abortion rights—actions that sparked internal controversy among group members. For a new organization with meager financial resources, the adoption of these two positions entailed significant costs. Since labor unions continued to withhold their support of the Equal Rights Amendment, for example, NOW's position on the matter deprived the group of the office space and printing and mailing facilities it had enjoyed courtesy of the United Auto Workers.[7] As a result, "NOW was forced to divert precious funds to renting an office in Washington, D.C., which it had trouble staffing."[8] Frustrated by NOW activists' embrace of the politically and socially controversial abortion issue, a group of NOW members soon defected to create their own organizations, the Women's Equity Action League (WEAL). WEAL founders argued that NOW's position on abortion undermined its ability to secure equal employment opportunities for women. WEAL constructed a less participatory and representative organizational structure and remained much more strategically limited than NOW.[9] Nevertheless, the two groups later worked together when it suited their mutual purposes.[10]

Tactics

The breadth of NOW's tactical repertoire is often overlooked.[11] To implement its Bill of Rights, NOW initially focused chiefly on institutionalized political channels and on networking inside and outside established governmental and nongovernmental organizations.[12] Friedan in particular urged NOW members to present NOW's Bill of Rights to those in political power; they were to "act to bring our Bill of Rights for Women in 1968 to the attention of local political representatives and candidates as well as to [their] representatives in Washington, and to devise new ways of exposing and combating sex discrimination in employment, education, the political parties, churches, and mass media." For their part, the national officers were charged with "urging support by appropriate officials of the executive and legislative branches of Government and other organizations, specifically the President of the United States and members of Congress and the State Commissions on the Status of Women, and by the Republican and Democratic parties by inclusion in their party platforms."[13]

Despite this focus on mainstream political institutions, Friedan and other founders clearly expected NOW to use a variety of tactics, including activating cross-organizational alliances, lobbying industry, holding demonstrations, and mobilizing the membership and the public to become involved in all these endeavors. NOW founders and members did not hesitate to participate in marches or picket lines.

Even before NOW's inception the *New York Times* reported that future NOW founder Pauli Murray urged women to protest actively: "If it becomes necessary to march on Washington to assure equal job opportunities for all, I hope women will not flinch from the thought."[14] When she first considered the kind of organization she wanted to lead, Friedan specifically embraced Murray's view, comparing the tactics employed by moderate women's groups such as the League of Women Voters and the American Association of University Women unfavorably with those used by fiery feminists of the suffrage period. Freeman notes, "Direct-action tactics, and NOW's other activities, were not just to catch the public eye but also to pressure the government. They were part of an overall campaign that also used letter writing, court suits, and meetings with government officials. Many early NOW members had engaged in lobbying for other groups, and it seemed perfectly logical to continue same types of activities for a new movement."[15]

Early examples of NOW's protest activity include its picketing of the *New York Times* in August 1967 due to its sex-segregated employment advertisements and its demonstrations in front of the offices of the Equal Employment Opportunity Commission to call attention to that body's unwillingness to deal with sex discrimination in the workplace.[16] In addition to demonstrations, in May 1968 NOW also called for a "Fast to Free Women from Poverty Day" during which "women around the country, rich and poor, black and white, will not eat for a day. . . . They'll give their grocery money for the day to the Poor People's Campaign. After all, 80 per cent of the poor are women."[17]

To highlight the need to desegregate public areas and to attract media attention, NOW members provoked owners of men's-only bars and restaurants by conducting "sit-ins"—albeit much less emotionally and physically dangerous ones than those held earlier by African Americans.[18] (The worst that happened to feminist protesters was having drinks poured on their heads.) In a similar bid for media time and new recruits, Friedan organized the "Women's Strike for Equality," a successful mass march and strike of women workers on August 26, 1970, timed to coincide with the fiftieth anniversary of women's suffrage.[19] NOW organized another mass demonstration to demand universal child care on Mother's Day, 1971.

President Friedan's report at NOW's March 1969 national board meeting clearly showed her interest in another tactic: participating in electoral politics. Friedan suggested that NOW join in an "alliance . . . to form a political power bloc for the attainment of specific goals, and the support of candidates pledged to work for NOW goals."[20] The board discussed the latter suggestion but decided that since voter mobilization remained key to success in the political arena, NOW should first focus on increasing its membership. Board members also sought reassurance that NOW intended to support men and women of either party, as long as they were sympathetic to NOW's agenda.[21]

In 1970 NOW encouraged members' direct participation in electoral politics: "Even when election appears unlikely, NOW members should run for office to educate the public about our concerns. Local chapters should encourage women already active in politics to run on women's issues. Local chapters should set up committees to seek out candidates. Regional conferences should include workshops to train prospective candidates and campaign workers."[22] The 1970 board also approved a resolution directing Friedan to hold a press conference to ask women to donate money or time only to candidates or parties supporting the ERA.[23]

NOW's national conventions echoed this awareness of the importance of the electoral arena: in 1971 the national conference theme was "From the Doll's House to the White House." In the same year, NOW also conducted schools for political candidates.[24] An invitation to these training sessions stated, "The National Organization for Women, in running the School for Candidates, believes a most effective rallying-cry to be RUNNING FOR POLITICAL OFFICE."[25] The chair of the Politics Task Force noted that this kind of activity "shows our obvious heavy focus on politics as a key means of getting women into the 'mainstream of American life' and more important, for changing the mainstream of American life. . . . During the last two years, the Politics Task Force has worked with hundreds of NOW members who have run for office."[26]

Early in its development, NOW worked with other women's organizations to enhance women's political influence and resources. A new bipartisan women's organization, the National Women's Political Caucus (NWPC), formed in 1971, as Janet Flammang notes, to "oppose racism, sexism, ageism, institutionalized violence, and poverty through the election and appointment of women to public office, party reform, and the support of women's issues and feminist candidates."[27] In contrast to NOW, the NWPC was widely known as the "political arm" of the women's movement. Friedan, Bella Abzug, Gloria Steinem, and Shirley Chisholm were among the founding members. Wilma Scott Heide (NOW President from 1971 to 1974) also joined the NWPC and worked with its leaders regularly. NOW national conferences resolved to support the goals of the NWPC, including the training of feminist candidates. In fact, many NOW members maintained their involvement in both organizations. Some of the NWPC's other goals that NOW supported in the 1971 National Conference were "forming women's caucuses within every party and every state; forming a caucus within every county in every party; forming a caucus within every congressional district in every party; ensuring that 50% of delegates to national conventions are women . . . teaching women through school for political candidates not only on the party ticket but elected in the primaries and later elected against the opposition candidates from major parties." A 1974 survey of NOW members (342 replies) found that 16% claimed membership in NWPC as well.[28]

Friedan and the national board quickly developed ties with groups such as the Leadership Council on Civil Rights, labor groups, and others sympathetic to women's issues in order to further their relationship with Washington politicians and to gain information and resources. In 1968 the NOW membership further resolved: "NOW will urge the Urban Coalition, the National Alliance for Businessmen and similar organizations to seek the participation and advice of women in an effort to deal with the problems of the hard core unemployed—the majority of whom in many communities are women—and to go to John Gardiner of the Urban Coalition and other appropriate officials to implement this."

From NOW's inception, involvement in political parties also claimed a notable share of the group's political effort. A 1970 conference resolution, for example, "called for the formation of women's rights caucuses within existing political parties and organizations as well as the establishment of independent women's political caucuses."[29] In 1971 NOW resolved to "insist on the inclusion of a women's rights plank in all party platforms and recommends that the NOW National board present our demands to the platform committees at the parties' national conventions."[30]

Forming connections with other activist and civil rights organizations constituted yet another important early tactic. In 1968, for example, NOW chapter leader Eliza Paschall initiated such a relationship in Atlanta with civil rights leaders who "helped plan NOW's participation in the Poor People's Campaign." NOW's newsletter reported this important liaison: "A major first has been scored by [the Georgia-Atlanta Chapter] in its success in forming an alliance between the female civil rights movement and the black civil rights movement and the beginning of a dialogue on the mutuality of the causes."[31]

In June 1969, at a meeting of the board, Friedan argued for an "alliance of NOW with other women's groups to form a political power block for the attainment of specific goals, and the support of candidates pledged to work for NOW goals."[32] The ensuing discussion, recorded in the minutes, suggested a great deal of support for such coalition work, even with more radically oriented groups: "The idea of seeking to form coalitions with other groups interested in various NOW goals was supported by most speakers, and comments were made that it would be possible to work with some 'radical' groups on the basis of selective coalition. It was suggested that a major purpose of conferences with other groups could be to identify areas of agreement and suggest ways to implement social change." Board members decided to cancel its scheduled September 1969 board meeting in order to host a meeting of organizations that might be interested in forming a coalition with NOW on one or more issues.[33]

The variety of organizations attending this conference (and others held at about the same time) underscores the interaction between NOW and a wide variety of groups. Attending the conference were representatives from the following organizations: Women's Liberation, Woman Power, Women Inc., Women's Caucus of the Berkeley Sociology Association, Women's City Club, Women for Peace, National Negro Business and Professional Women, Daughters of Bilitis, Women's Bureau of the U.S. Department of Labor, Delta Sigma Theta Sorority, Soroptimist Club of San Francisco, Society for Humane Abortions, California Institute of the Arts, Young Socialists Alliance, Negro Historical and Cultural Society, Student Mobilization Committee, Mexican-American Political Association, California Committee to Legalize Abortions, American Association of University Women, Business and Professional Women, Women's International League for Peace and Freedom, and Socialist Workers Party. Representatives reached agreement on the need for child-care centers, on the importance of "establishing a continuing communication network between women's organizations on issues pertinent to their membership and convening another coalition meeting within a few months," on women's reproductive rights, on the need to cooperate to combat workplace discrimination against women, and on the "promotion of women's caucuses in the unions, professions and political parties." The November 1969 Congress to Unite Women, for example, brought together many radical women's liberation groups in a national coalition. At the meeting, "five hundred women, including representatives of 25 chapters of 15 different organizations from Massachusetts to Maryland," adopted resolutions to cooperate to pursue the creation of twenty-four-hour day-care centers, abortion law reform, and the ERA.[34] In her December 1969 report to the board, Friedan concluded, "The regional conferences held during the fall were a major NOW effort and were successful in bringing together various groups and individuals involved in the women's liberation movement."[35] Her phrasing suggests that by the end of 1969 the National Organization for Women identified itself as a bona fide member of the "radical" branch of the women's rights movement.

The Evolution of NOW's Early Strategic Focus

One of NOW's earliest targets, inducing the EEOC to address employment discrimination against women, remained unsatisfied. Four years after NOW's inception the secretary of labor "concede[d] job discrimination against women is 'subtle and more pervasive' than against minority groups but [said the] labor department [would] not take immediate action to combat it."[36] As a result of this gridlock, many activists felt that a stronger statement of NOW's strategy and vision for the future were necessary:[37]

> NOW's strategy, particularly in the areas of protest, legislation and litigation—has leaned heavily on the experience of the black civil rights struggle. What we borrowed from the blacks—the peaceful protests, the legislative lobbying, the pressure on employers and educators, the filing of complaints and lawsuits—has helped us win a seriousness, even awe, for our organization. . . . But we in NOW must realize that the black struggle has accomplished no real revolution, that in some ways it is only just discovering itself, that we must not be trapped in the same pitfalls, and that we are at a point of departure from it and from all others. Thus, the need to develop new, more effective strategy.[38]

Frustration with its progress on some of its primary goals spurred NOW's outreach to newer women's liberation groups. NOW thus looked increasingly to the activities of the newer civil rights and women's groups that followed it.

Many of the early radical women's groups formed in New York, among them New York Radical Women (NYRW). Over time the membership of the NYRW and the New York NOW chapter overlapped. NYRW, created in a split from the New Left organization Students for a Democratic Society, is credited with introducing the tactic of consciousness-raising (C-R).[39] This method of small group discussion drew new individuals into activism by facilitating their discovery of the social construction of their problems.

NOW chapter leaders quickly absorbed the tactics of women's liberation activists. Freeman argues that new NOW members demanded this activity: "It was with great reluctance that many NOW chapters set them up to 'cater' to the needs of their newest members. The idea . . . was contrary to NOW's image of itself as an action organization."[40] NOW's emphasis on action rather than education, however, had undermined its ability to incorporate members into the group's decision-making structure, as Clarenbach noted:

> Many members are seeking information and are not on a very sophisticated wavelength. This has implications for total focus and emphasis of NOW. Our Statement of Purpose is not enough for those members rather new to the subject. Education of NOW members through our organization must be part of our program. . . . More guidance on issues and action items is an apparent need of some local chapters. Where a national board member can be present at each chapter meeting this problem is minimized, but a national director is not always available.[41]

C-R proved to be a useful tactic. It supported NOW's goals but did not require a large investment of resources. C-R groups attracted new members and became a means of educating and activating them at the same time. As Kathie Sarachild characterizes C-R, that is exactly its purpose: to "get to the most radical truths about the situation of women in order to take radical action . . . learning the truth can lead to all kinds of action and this action will lead to further truths." It allowed women at the local level to discover the issues that most concerned them and then to decide the actions best suited to addressing those issues.[42] In NOW its use became widespread just as the group experienced a surge in new members in 1970.[43] Consciousness-raising became one of the few formal means of educating NOW members.

NOW's strategy also evolved to incorporate other methods employed by women's liberation activists. Tactically speaking, radical women's liberation groups favored the "politics of protest," which Sidney Tarrow defines as "the use of disruptive collective action aimed at institutions, elites, authorities and other groups, on behalf of the actors or of those they claim to represent."[44] Women's liberation groups waged demonstrations, picketed, took over bureaucratic offices and made demands on officials, and performed street theater to bring to the attention of passers-by the absurdity of women's status in American society. Soon national NOW and many NOW chapters were comfortable employing the same tactics, often side by side with more "radical" organizations.

The women's liberation movement also encouraged another shift in NOW strategy: the acceptance of lesbian rights. When Betty Friedan exited as NOW's first president in 1970 after four years of leadership, NOW's commitment to lesbian rights remained unresolved. Friedan's outspoken opposition to this goal and her association with a purge of lesbians from a New York chapter contributed to the volatility of the issue within the group. Leaders more sympathetic to the concerns of lesbians succeeded Friedan, including former EEOC commissioner Aileen Hernandez and Wilma Scott Heide, who took office in September 1971.[45] At their 1971 national conference NOW members finally formally acknowledged the legitimacy of lesbian rights as a feminist issue. Two years later NOW set up its first task force on the subject.

From 1966 to 1971 NOW became more open to "radical" tactics and goals, but the roots of many of the changes it made are evident in the values and experiences of the founders and first members. NOW's early commitment to being on the vanguard of the feminist movement and to urging women to take action on their own behalf undoubtedly eased this transition. Members willingly participated in sit-ins, lobbying campaigns, and consciousness-raising sessions. NOW's 1966 Statement of Purpose focused on the rights and needs of women in traditional marriages, but by 1971 the group had begun to expand its conception of gender and its influence on sexuality, relationships, and families.

Between 1972 and 1978, as the radical women's liberation movement declined (indeed, New York Radical Women did not last two years), the National Organization for Women emerged as a fixture in American politics. As NOW activists considered and implemented organizational and strategic changes during this time, they remained committed to the principles and practices laid out in the governance structure the group had forged during its founding period.

4. Out of the Mainstream, into the Revolution?

The Legacy of NOW's Guiding Principles, 1972–1978

Must we imitate the systems of the oppressor?

Lois Galgay Reckitt

Between 1972 and 1978 NOW reached a second stage of development. As Ronald Hrebenar notes, "eventually some social movements evolve into political interest groups with a well-defined membership, regular funding, a permanent staff, and knowledge on how
to operate within the political system."[1] NOW's halting steps toward
committing to a new strategy—the campaign to ratify the Equal
Rights Amendment—and the expansion of its electoral activities
seem emblematic of this transformation. Some scholars maintain
that as collective action organizations become formalized and institutionalized, ties between leaders and members weaken, prompting
members to withdraw support from these organizations. For example, Michael Goldfield argues in his study of the decline of organized labor that "overall . . . the bureaucratization of U.S. unions
begun in the late thirties stifled opposition, dissent, and much rank-
and-file initiative."[2]

The development of the National Organization for Women did
not follow this pattern of diminishing member support.[3] As NOW

continued to routinize its procedures and professionalize its national office, its focus on remaining at the forefront of women's rights issues, to sustaining grassroots activism, to pursuing a multi-issue and multitactical strategy, to the preservation of its political independence, and to action remained central concerns of members and leaders.

Many NOW leaders believed that political conditions favored making the ERA and electoral activism organizational priorities. Yet, others persistently questioned this strategy, believing it undermined rather than reflected and supported NOW's governance structure.

NOW's "Second Stage"

Between 1966 and 1971 the National Organization for Women created a template for its values and practices, began to form task forces to investigate women's issues, created chapters, and established a regional structure. The group took bold positions, held press conferences, led demonstrations, attracted significant media attention, forged connections with other civil rights and women's liberation organizations, pressured politicians, worked to allow women into male-only bastions, and lobbied to end discrimination against women in the workplace.

The political environment of the early 1970s induced cautious optimism among women's rights advocates. Nixon vetoed the Comprehensive Child Care Act in late 1971 and won reelection in 1972, but other events favored feminist goals. Representative Shirley Chisholm's presidential candidacy, the national Democratic convention's amenability to feminist issues and to the inclusion of female delegates, and a promising election year all constituted significant political opportunities for women in 1972.

In a memo to board members and others in 1972, the chair of the Politics Task Force emphasized NOW's participation at both the Democratic and Republican national conventions. "As you can see from watching the news, our impact is being felt enormously in the pre-convention committees of rules, credentials and platform . . . we have been working at committee hearings—and behind the scenes—with NOW members, members of NWPC, and Planned Parenthood."[4] The Supreme Court's *Roe v. Wade* decision in January 1973 was also a major victory for feminists.

In 1974 NOW and other feminist organizations celebrated as they were invited to a meeting with President Ford—the first time any president had consented to such a meeting. The same year, Mary Louise Smith, a longtime GOP activist, party co-chair, and member of NOW and the NWPC, rose to the chairmanship of the Republican National Committee.[5] NOW's board endorsed its first political candidate, voting to support Bella Abzug in the New York Democratic primary for the U.S. Senate, "contingent on endorsement of New York State NOW," voting 23 in favor, 2 against, 4 abstaining. The following day, five members revoked their support for the measure, but the resolution prevailed.[6] The board resolved that the Task Force on Politics formulate guidelines for future endorsements.[7]

In 1975 Congress passed a minimum wage bill. The passage of the Educational Equity Act and of anti–pregnancy discrimination initiatives, as well as FCC license revocations for discriminatory hiring, also counted as important wins for feminist organizations. NOW participated in many of these issues, largely through the work of its legislative vice president, who developed the group's lobbying capabilities, opening a legislative office at the outset of the 93d Congress.[8]

Yet in terms of tangible policy results, NOW could boast few true victories. NOW sought to confront targets that would mobilize its membership, show its political clout, and establish itself as a serious, powerful component of the political landscape. Moreover, the group's financial situation remained highly unstable, aggravated by the fact that its ability to reach out to new members or communicate efficiently with current members lagged far behind demand. Among NOW's foremost tasks in this period was to regularize its financial situation, which depended almost exclusively on the members. Founders and board members still paid for many expenses, including travel and phone calls, out of their own pockets. NOW also had to continue work on producing information and disseminating it to members and chapters while attracting new recruits.

Financial Challenges

NOW's ongoing financial difficulties hampered its establishment of necessary organizational routines. Task forces, for example, NOW's main engine for research on new issues and tactical development, remained seriously underfunded. Without adequate resources, NOW's regional structure also struggled to fulfill their purpose of integrating members and chapters across the country. NOW's national newsletter advised potential candidates for the board or for national office that they must expect to shoulder some expenses.[9]

Relief was slow in coming. Magnifying the organization's financial problems, several chapters began withholding dues from national NOW in 1973. Chapters intended to express their dissatisfaction with the services provided by national NOW and, later on, to convey their reservations regarding the integrity of the group's leadership. The resulting internal dissension eroded NOW's ability to attract external donations.[10]

In response, the national office took steps to reduce expenses. The monthly newsletter, *DO IT NOW*, became bimonthly and began to carry paid advertising. All expense items for the 1975 budget were cut "to minimum survival appropriations."[11] National NOW warned chapters that they could expect only minimal assistance with their administrative tasks, with "information supply," and with their lobbying activities.[12]

Distributing Power and Implementing Principles

In 1973, largely to address its problems of information processing, NOW leaders created both a public information office in New York City and an administrative national headquarters in Chicago. In addition to systematizing the provision of information to the public, these offices were designed to help national leaders venture out in the field more often to meet with local leaders, facilitating communication with the grass roots about national initiatives and priorities.

NOW members sought to boost grassroots influence despite the fact that local chapters enjoyed a great deal of autonomy. In 1973 the New York and California NOW chapters demanded that national leaders implement a major change in the organization's structure: the formal recognition of a state level. They voted to withhold dues until NOW agreed to remand certain percentage of such dues to support the state-level.[13] The director of the Eastern Region from 1971 to 1974 wrote to President Heide, "I believe state organization is the trend of NOW for the future, and a very healthy trend, and I feel national must give this trend more recognition, funds, etc. rather than ignore it. [The withholding of dues] represents I believe a sign of real and continued dissatisfaction with national, especially concerning the service the national office gives for the dues."[14]

Despite these changes, NOW activists continued to pressure the national level for further reforms. For their part, some frustrated NOW leaders felt that members mistakenly viewed the national office as a domineering "mother" seeking to control her "children." Pleading with members to recognize the limitations of national's power—and the need to strengthen rather than weaken it—in 1973 in her address at the California state conference, Vice President Toni Carabillo reminded activists that NOW comprised

> 600 chapters which cannot be commanded, but only invited, to provide the essential support and follow-through, and who may, at the critical time, be absorbed in significant projects of their own. . . . National is fewer than a half-dozen full-time employees (all of whom were hired less than a year ago) in three different cities trying to be responsive to 13 national officers, 25 national board members, 30 national task force coordinators and members of all 600 chapters. National is a Public Information Office and a Legislative Lobbying Office in their respective cubby-holes in New York and Washington, functioning on a total budget—for salaries and operations—of 20,000 each. . . . National is not, in short, "them"—it's "us" out of town.

An organizational innovation demanded by sub-national units, the incorporation of a state structure added a bureaucratic layer to the group not to insulate leaders from members but to amplify participation and representation within it. Supporters of the change expected that a state structure would improve communication between chapters and the national level of the organization, and they argued that it would foster greater independence and strength at the local level. Other demands for reform followed: at the national conference in 1975, members voted to hold a bylaws convention in the following year to consider creating a system of delegate voting. To this point in NOW's history, only members attending annual conferences were eligible to vote on NOW's policies and priorities. A delegate system, reformers hoped, would improve the representation of NOW's increasingly geographically diverse membership.

Following a contentious internal election in October 1975, the national board commenced work on provisions intended to convince members of the national level's responsiveness to their concerns, their adherence to the group's guiding principles, and their eagerness to share power. To accomplish these tasks the board approved several new initiatives. First, the board resolved to increase its financial support for task forces and for the projects they generated, especially for those featuring action-oriented components. In addition, "approximately 20%" of all national dues would be fed back into state organizations. Second, national leaders voted to clarify their intentions with respect to the ERA campaign. They maintained that no state would be compelled to work on behalf of the Equal Rights Amendment. National officers pledged to consult and coordinate with states prior to embarking on ERA projects. As Beverly Jones, chair of the Committee on Board Organization, explained:

> We passed a measure which placed the authority and the responsibility for developing strategy to pass the ERA in the hands of those state organizations in the unratified states which must themselves do the work necessary for ratification. That measure explicitly defines the role of the national organization as one of unstinting support. The national organization will offer whatever funds and expertise it can muster and permit the unratified states to draw on these resources in whatever manner they, themselves, deem helpful and appropriate.[15]

To pay for these provisions, the board axed its recently created public information office as well as the national office's Chicago arm. Emphasizing the need for these reforms, Jones said, "Most of us

on the board ran for election on a platform that advocated greater
autonomy for chapter and state organizations. . . . No uniform program at the national level can possibly encompass all of our differences, and the price of attempting to enforce a unitary program on a
large and unwilling segment of the membership is alienation, fac-
tionalization, splits and decay."[16]

Notwithstanding the implementation of measures enhancing local
power, many activists remained apprehensive about the resources national NOW leaders were committing to the ERA's passage. Focusing
on this single issue undermined the group's commitment to press for
change on a wide range of feminist concerns and its obligation to take
account of the interests of local activists. Midwest regional director
Mary Anne Sedey brandished the 1976 budget to make the point: "Excluding ERA funds, only [$]147,500 of NOW's million dollar projected
budget is allocated for NOW's program (14.4%). How is this consistent with the objectives of the National Organization for Women?"[17]

National NOW leaders attempted to reassure members that
NOW's structure of revenue distribution, in contrast to that of nearly
all other major women's groups, indeed reflected the organization's
principles:

> Both LWV [League of Women Voters] and BPW [Business and Profes-
> sional Women] claim to have raised over [$]100,000 each on this issue
> [the ERA]. However, NOW is the only organization to have provided
> direct cash aids to its subunits in unratified states to use in accordance
> with their individually developed ratification plans. This is a depar-
> ture from the usual pattern of "maternalism" by national organiza-
> tions, since it represents a means of providing a support system by uti-
> lizing the national organization merely as a conduit and collection
> agent for getting money directly to the grass roots. We think our mem-
> bers should know that in fund raising, as in all else, we seek nontradi-
> tional approaches to solving old problems in new ways freed of con-
> straints inherent in patriarchal systems.[18]

A new mobilization of politically conservative groups increasingly
jeopardized the ERA's probability of success as the decade pro-

gressed, bolstering leaders' arguments that NOW should make the campaign a top priority. Yet others countered that NOW's commitment to a diverse set of goals remained critical precisely because conservative groups intended not only to prevent the ERA's passage but also to block or reverse progress on other feminist issues. As a result, local activists and leaders, as well as national board members, cautioned that NOW must remain active in seeking equality for lesbians, the elimination of poverty and racism, the pursuit of full reproductive rights for women, the achievement of equality in broadcasting and media, and in ending sexual violence against women.

Once again, leaders' attempts to mitigate activists' complaints, such as their directive to regional directors asking them to "hold a meeting of State Coordinators and board members from their regions to implement the will of chapters . . . and to supply input on state needs to board members," proved inadequate. The meetings revealed that many remained convinced that NOW's decision-making structure required more fundamental reforms. For example, recounting events at a gathering of Midwest state coordinators, Sedey noted: "The group passed fifteen motions, most involving power-related matters. For example, the group requested clarification as to how appointments to task forces and board committees were determined (i.e. whether the president receives input on these appointments) and asked that national leaders desist from releasing press statements and from meeting with the media without first consulting regional and chapter leaders."[19]

In this context, among the most significant changes ratified by members at NOW's 1976 bylaws convention were election reforms that redistributed power among the national, regional, and state levels of the organization. Enhancing the accountability of national board members to local activists, they would now be elected by members at regional, rather than national conferences. Regional directors, however, lost their automatic status as national officers. As a result, NOW's executive leadership cohort shrank to five officers from the original thirteen. Ellie Smeal remembers, "Marguerite Rawalt [a lawyer active in BPW] drafted the first bylaws. When the Majority Caucus won in 1975, the structure changed entirely from a traditional women's organization to a new type . . . from an elite band to a grassroots organization."[20]

NOW activists worked to align the group's decision-making structure with its principles. Underscoring the point, in a statement in favor of the proposed bylaws changes, activists Sandy Roth and Lillian Waugh contended: "This year in hearings around the country, you demanded the decentralization of the organization; the streamlining of internal operations; the development of a fiscally sound organization; the return of power to the membership through leadership accountability; and the creation of a flexible structure, able to respond quickly to demands of growth and change."[21]

Leadership Crises

Serious conflicts over the distribution of power arose not only between NOW's national and local levels but also among national officers, board members, and task force leaders. A series of fractious board meetings prompted one distressed board member to write in 1973:

> What is bothering the board of NOW is a power struggle. That power struggle involved the question of who shall run NOW and how. Some of the issues are ideological . . . and some are about power—e.g. whose project shall have how much funding, who shall make critical decisions, etc. . . . It is a matter of applying our principles of fair play, openness and democracy to our practices in our organization.[22]

Discord among national officers and board members engendered two opposing factions. One (whose goals were later incorporated into a group calling itself "Womansurge"), argued against the creation of a state structure and the institutionalization of a delegate system for voting in national elections. These changes, they contended, promised to add confusing layers of bureaucracy between the grass roots and the national office, making it more difficult for individuals to exert influence within NOW. Deradicalization would result. Activist Lois Galgay Reckitt (composer of the official "con" statement against the proposed bylaws changes) asked, "Must we imitate the systems of the oppressor?"

Although the bylaws were ratified overwhelmingly, opponents represented a significant minority within the organization; in fact, their ranks included at least five national leaders. Perceiving themselves "as radicals," they declared they "would leave the mainstream—and if it caught up with us, we would leave again."[23]

In addition to protesting bylaws changes, Womansurge insisted that NOW's task forces and the group's initiatives needed to reflect more accurately the interests of members. They argued that chapters required greater autonomy and power in addition to an increased financial allotment from the national level and sought to curtail the national level's habit of initiating new programs (or "actions") before determining the preferences of local activists. Womansurge pointed out that the national body often neglected to provide chapters with adequate lead time or resources to carry out national action plans.[24]

Finally, this faction advocated against investing more of NOW's resources in the mainstream political process. Invoking the organization's principles, the group protested that participating in campaign and party politics was incompatible with maintaining NOW's social change agenda. The tactic served, not to mobilize or empower masses of women, but to elevate the public status of a few officers.

In contrast, a second leadership faction calling itself the "Majority Caucus" favored the development of a robust state level. At the same time, the majority caucus maintained that NOW's progress depended on reinforcing the national level's ability to lead the organization. The passage of the Equal Rights Amendment, for example, required efficient coordination of activity and information at both state and national levels.

In addition, the Majority Caucus argued that political conditions demanded that NOW increase its visibility and participation in electoral politics. Charlene Suneson, NOW's national secretary, Majority Caucus member, and political specialist, asserted that simply lobbying legislators for their vote would not secure the ratification of the ERA. Instead, the key to success was NOW's participation in electoral campaigns. The Majority Caucus claimed that it did not subscribe to an oligarchic, elitist, or conservative ethic despite its proposals to strengthen the national office and to work in electoral campaigns. Rather, these positions represented an extension of the participatory, radical, and grassroots-oriented goals and tactics that NOW members expected. A delegate system would not undermine NOW's democratic practices but enhance them by ensuring that members from chapters around the country (not just those who lived near the area where the annual conference was held) would have a voice. DeCrow emphasized, "I stated, very clearly, all along, that what I wanted to do was not enter the mainstream in full partnership with men, but to change the mainstream."[25]

The fissures among national NOW leaders grew more pronounced between 1974 and 1976 as they vied against each other in divisive national elections for officers and board members. Karen DeCrow, in many ways a transitional figure who attempted to keep the peace between factions, was elected president in 1974 under the pro–Majority Caucus slogan "Out of the Mainstream Into the Revolution!" The slogan represented the caucus's belief that mainstream political tactics could be effectively employed in the pursuit of radical social, economic, and political goals.

In response to the Majority Caucus platform in 1975, a group dubbing itself the Seattle Ad Hoc Committee scorned the caucus's rationalizations, noting, "We are not even clear about their platform; it seems fraught with inconsistencies. They say 'out of the mainstream,' while insisting that NOW endorse and work for political candidates. They say 'into the revolution,' while arguing that NOW should extend its appeal to housewives and working women."[26] For many NOW members, the concept of bringing women in general or NOW as an organization into the "mainstream" was at best an uninspiring and at worst a highly suspect strategy. As activist Reckitt noted, the debate over outsider/insider goals and tactics remained "the crux of the controversy that enveloped NOW for the next ten years."[27]

Attempting to soothe intraorganizational divisions, national

NOW suggested in national newsletters that despite the controversies, the factions had resolved their major differences and were ready to move forward. President DeCrow reassured members that the 1976 bylaws conference would reaffirm NOW's principles and allow the embattled organization to right itself: "Raising consciousness, through formal and informal education, will of course be one of the conference goals. . . . Our conference will begin with actions and with workshops. There will be no plenary sessions until Saturday. . . . It is time, as we approach NOW's Tenth Anniversary, as the nation celebrates its bicentennial, and as the world celebrates international women's year, to strengthen our ideology and galvanize into meaningful, feminist action."[28]

National NOW also expressed concern for the membership preferences by surveying members regarding the group's priorities. The survey asked whether and to what extent NOW should address issues such as women in advertising; housing; employment and economic security; health care; food production, distribution, costs, and quality; national energy production and distribution; worker layoffs due to economic crisis; child-care funding; eliminating rape; and the criminal justice system.

Such national-level initiatives failed to resolve outstanding conflicts over strategy and tactics. Still looming prominently was the question of how NOW could seek political influence without becoming co-opted and elite-driven. The Seattle Ad Hoc Committee warned:

> Our overriding concerns internally at this point at [NOW's] constitutional convention [include] the question of political endorsement, and whether the board will be responsive to the membership. . . . Political endorsement is to us an unresolved issue, although it does not seem to be to the Majority Caucus. All three workshops held on this issue at the Philadelphia conference indicated strong disagreement in this organization over whether political endorsement should occur at all. Implementation was never discussed because of this basic difference. In the second workshop, a straw vote strongly opposed national endorsements (including U.S. Senators and Reps.) and at the local level,

our chapters span the political gamut from socialists to Republicans. Endorsement decisions would be highly divisive. But this issue never came to the floor of the conference. Seattle NOW has voted unanimously to oppose political endorsement. WE feel that involving NOW in the political process *in this way* jeopardizes the very nature and effectiveness of the organization.[29]

Prevailing in the face of such objections, the Majority Caucus took office and began to press its agenda. They immediately intensified NOW's activity on behalf of the ERA.[30] Although misgivings over NOW's political participation persisted among both rank and file activists and some board members, a majority of NOW members consistently voted at national conferences to support both the Majority Caucus as well as its strategic vision. At the 1977 national conference in Detroit, members approved by a narrow margin the creation of an institutionalized interest group's ultimate weapon—a political action committee.[31]

The ERA Strategy and the Legacy of NOW's Guiding Principles

The successful movement of the ERA out of the Senate to the states for ratification also buoyed feminist spirits.[32] In the early 1970s NOW leaders felt convinced of the ERA's success. One longtime activist remembered: "The 1973 convention, the first since the ERA was sent to the states . . . had only one workshop on the ERA—and it didn't even have a write-up in the post-convention summaries. We were that confident."[33]

This confidence began to be shaken by mid-1973.[34] At the same time, some NOW leaders began to grasp the utility of the Equal Rights Amendment ratification campaign as a tool for recruitment and organizational development. In 1973 Eastern regional director Jacqueline Ceballos wrote to Jo Ann Evans Gardner that NOW members "have really organized around the ERA . . . and we now have a state organization and 14 new NOW chapters just because of the fight for ERA. I wonder will we ever have as strong an issue to organize around."[35] NOW's involvement included resolving to lobby the Democratic and Republican national conventions to ensure that the parties supported the ERA in their platforms.[36] By 1976 the ERA campaign figured increasingly prominently in NOW's participation in national party politics.[37]

Yet NOW's leaders remained sensitive to the unease with which members often greeted such forays into "establishment" politics. Throughout the ERA effort, NOW members and some leaders expressed reservations that fell into three (sometimes overlapping) categories. Each objection hinged upon the way the campaign could impact NOW's principles and the integrity of its decision-making processes.

Primarily, members felt that the ERA and the mainstream political activities the campaign entailed threatened to undermine NOW's commitment to grassroots mobilizing. Second, the ERA strategy eroded NOW's position as an outsider in the system and its commitment to representing the vanguard of feminist activism. Finally, the strategy threatened NOW's ability to maintain its political independence.

Although they accepted the legitimacy of some participation in mainstream activities such as legislative lobbying and legal action, activists often expressed reservations about excessive involvement in purely "political" activities. Their hesitation constrained NOW leaders' ability to fully focus on the ERA strategy.

For example, a 1973 memo by Politics Task Force chair Suneson proposing the creation of a "temporary political device" or "political action arm" pledged that such a vehicle would be used only for a specific purpose, the ERA, after which it would be dissolved. In addition to carefully outlining the terms of the device's dissolution, Suneson's memo affirmed that the political action committee's governance structure would mirror NOW's own.

Anticipating the skepticism her proposal would receive, Suneson noted, "It undoubtedly will be wondered if there is a hidden agenda to this proposal, if it is a grab for internal power in NOW, etc. IT IS NOT. I personally have been a federal government employee since 1954 and am precluded from direct political action by the Hatch Act."[38] Electoral political activity and the ERA ratification campaign appeared to redistribute power and resources to the national level of NOW. To her dismay, Suneson found that her assurances failed to disarm critics:

> I have had a couple communications that indicate there is some mis-understanding about the political device. It has not been put forth be-cause I or anyone else "likes" political action. My own involvement in NOW has been entirely legislative. Where legislative action can ac-complish ratification of the ERA there is no reason to bring in politi-cal action. However, various state ERA coordinators have indicated they do not believe legislative action alone will ratify the ERA.[39]

Suneson doggedly argued that the political realities of the ERA battle made it necessary to "facilitat[e] the removal of anti-ERA state legislators from office in unratified states." She noted that the ERA had already failed "by a large margin" in some states: "The ERA was solidly defeated in each of these states even though NOW has reasonable strength and organization in the majority of these states." Aware that anti-ERA groups, working with conservative and reli-gious organizations, were effectively countering feminist lobbying ef-forts, Suneson warned:

> There is no known basis for any belief that continued sole use of leg-islative tactics will produce anything different in the future than it did in 1973 in these states. A substantial number of the 18 ERA coordinators from unratified states present at the ERA colloquium in May 1973 indi-cated essentially that the legislators in their states did know and under-stand that opposition to the ERA was ill founded & often from out of state, and regardless of any grass roots pro-ERA sentiment were simply anti-ERA and no amount of lobbying or grassroots support would change this. The only effective action left was to remove anti-ERA legis-lators from office. . . . In view of the critical nature of the 1974 election, such direct political action must be started immediately.[40]

The possibility that the ERA might eclipse all other NOW issues and increase the power of national leaders vis-à-vis chapters and members set a significant proportion of NOW's members on edge. The ERA campaign and the tactics employed on its behalf also distressed those who felt the strategy symbolized the fact that the organization was no longer "theirs":

> For many of us this resolution [calling for NOW's full commitment to the ERA campaign] represented our fears that a centralized monolith would indeed be created under Ellie's direction—with little accountability to the membership. . . . In addition, we feared that all other issues would be neglected in favor of ERA. This was a particular concern of the Lesbian Caucus in NOW. However, on the floor of the Convention few delegates dared stand up and vote against the rhetoric as well as the legitimate arguments centered around the success of [one such team]. . . .[41]

The rising centrality of the ERA issue within NOW also provoked concern among members because the enormity of the task required coalition work with organizations such as ERAmerica and the National Women's Political Caucus. Participation in such coalitions diverted precious funds from other priorities. In addition, the positions and strategic preferences of other organizations in such coalitions often proved objectionable to NOW activists.[42] These problems underscored the way the exigencies of the ERA campaign occasionally undermined local preferences and prerogatives.[43]

In the discussion over Smeal's proposal to form ERA "strike forces" three years later, members repeatedly demanded to know whether all forms of protest activity were to be encouraged or whether the strike forces constituted simply another "mainstream political tool."[44] One activist argued that "the strategy of going around and sending a strike team to hold tea parties with these legislators [who] turn around and vote down the ERA, and vote down the ERA, has got to be questioned. I think we need to be out on the streets."[45] Another maintained that the real debate was "over whether to continue relying on politicians to solve and to win women's rights, or whether to build a vast feminist movement."[46]

Other skeptics argued that participating in partisan politics would lead NOW to abandon its commitment to representing the vanguard of the feminist movement. Their predictions were not without merit. The desire to win electoral majorities can encourage political moderation. In fact, as its investment in the ERA campaign increased over time, NOW also began working more visibly (testifying before Congress, for example) on less controversial issues such as the fate of displaced homemakers and the equal allocation of Social Security benefits. These actions on the part of chapters and national NOW reflected the recommendations of those working on NOW's public relations. Esther Kaw, vice president of public relations in 1976, underscored the fact that "NOW's goals for the next two years included providing technical and informational assistance to NOW chapters and task forces and encouraging greater involvement in NOW by women who are not, for the most part, aligned with the feminist movement (homemakers, older women, minority women, office workers, rural women, teachers)."[47]

Political involvement also dismayed NOW members who feared that because of such participation the group would stray from its principles by identifying itself with one party. A creeping partisanship seemed to loom as NOW campaigned heavily for pro-ERA Republican Gary Myers in his bid for a seat in the Virginia House against the anti-ERA Democratic incumbent in 1977 and as it increasingly castigated Democratic president Jimmy Carter for his marginal support of feminist concerns. NOW leaders repeatedly stressed the nonpartisan nature of NOW's involvement at board meetings and national conventions. NOW's refusal to endorse presidential candidates (a rule the group disregarded only once, in 1984) reinforced its nonpartisan stance.

NOW members urging restraint in electoral involvement also reminded members and leaders that even when "their" candidate emerged victorious, the newly elected official frequently reneged on promises made to support the feminist agenda. Activists often mentioned Florida and Nevada, where NOW activists' time, money, and energy were spent on election campaigns for candidates who subsequently failed to support NOW positions. In some cases, NOW chapters had compromised their strategic plans to cooperate with more moderate members of lobbying coalitions that hoped (in vain) thereby to gain one party's commitment for the ERA.

The resolution to establish a PAC carefully justified its roots in NOW history. Nevertheless, emphasizing the contentiousness of the tactic, just a few months after the conference, however, the Northwest Region passed a resolution (which they attempted to have adopted at a national board meeting) exhorting NOW to abstain from increased political action, echoing many of the reservations voiced at the national conference in April regarding NOW's deepening involvement in political affairs. Debaters considering whether or not NOW should create a political action committee questioned whether (1) NOW would be duped by politicians who appropriated the group's resources without intending to support its issues after the election; (2) NOW would be co-opted by party organizations; (3) such action would alienate NOW members not of the endorsed party; (4) other feminist organizations (such as the Women's Political Caucus) whose main goal was to support women's candidates would be weakened; and finally (5) increasing involvement in electoral campaigns would hinder NOW's lobbying efforts. Those supporting the resolution focused on the political "realities" and the fact that electoral politics was not a new dimension in NOW's tactical repertoire.

Even as Smeal and the Majority Caucus contended that a full-force electoral strategy was critical to the ERA's ratification, NOW continued to employ a diverse array of tactics and to address a wide range of feminist issues. National NOW encouraged chapters to decide for themselves the best way to work on the ERA project: "Each chapter must and should do what it believes best to pass the Equal Rights Amendment. No one is wiser than you in your chapters. You know your people. You set your strategy. You make your decision to do . . . whatever and wherever you feel will pass the ERA. . . . Whether you wish to quietly lobby . . . whether you wish to participate only at home in your area. These will be your decisions. The choice will be yours. You are wise."[48] As failures of ratification attempts around the country mounted and precious resources were expended to battle rescission attempts, national NOW leaders became convinced that they required more authority within the organization to coordinate these battles. Despite national's earlier assurances to chapters that they would maintain complete control of national's involvement in their states, when a 1977 (member-approved) resolution established Smeal's proposed strike forces, responsibility for this campaign shifted from states and regions to the national level. NOW increased its efforts to dethrone anti-ERA state legislators, targeting those who reneged on earlier promises to support the measure, proclaiming, "No Turncoat Will Return."

The years 1978–82 marked NOW's long-overdue (according to some) prioritization of the ratification campaign. President Smeal announced an ERA "State of Emergency," calling for the group to devote itself entirely to the issue. Given this urgent commitment, approved by the membership at the 1978 and 1980 national conventions, it is reasonable to expect that the group's four-year campaign would dramatically reshape the organization. In many ways, it did: as a result of the ERA drive, for example, NOW's membership increased to more than 200,000 people and its budget swelled to over $8 million. What was constant throughout the ERA "emergency" is how sensitive NOW members and leaders remained to the organization's guiding principles and practices.

5. The ERA "Emergency"

And Whereas, in light of these dire developments,
NOW cannot remain on the sidelines.

National NOW Times, October/November 1980

The years 1978–82 marked the National Organization for Women's full commitment to the ERA strategy. The details of the campaign have been well documented elsewhere.[1] Here I show that even when NOW leaders and members appeared to be in agreement about the wisdom of departing from the organization's guiding principles—devoting the vast bulk of the group's resources on a strategy that entailed focusing on a limited goal and a set of mainstream political tactics—they both continued to express the continuing importance of working within the constraints of NOW's governance structure. NOW Board resolutions approved during these final years of the ERA campaign confirm that the campaign to ratify the ERA did not fundamentally undermine the organization's commitment to principles such as grassroots activism and participation and to a multi-issue, multitactical strategy.

In 1978 NOW president Ellie Smeal persuaded the organization to declare an ERA "state of emergency." The resolution vowed to devote the energy of its 100,000 members and its $2 million budget to the ratification campaign.[2] (At the time of her announcement the deadline for ratification was March 22, 1979; later Congress extended the deadline to June 30, 1982.) The emergency declaration emphasized the need to lobby for an extension of the ERA deadline in order to take advantage of election cycles.[3] In a speech at NOW's 1978 National Conference Smeal declared that women's issues had finally emerged as vital to the political calculations of those seeking or holding office. She boasted, "In the last 18 months we have become a political movement in every state of this nation."[4]

Two years later, at the 1980 National Conference, NOW members voted for "total ERA mobilization," which called for increasing the size, diversity, and range of the ERA ratification campaign: "[NOW] pledges the development of at least three major projects the size of the 1980 Illinois campaign, continuing drives to stop rescission, development of new techniques of creative nonviolent protest, maximum use of NOW resources across the country, and vigorous pursuit of legal cases on the ERA Extension/Rescission and the Boycott."[5] Former NOW president Betty Friedan declared, "If we do not get Illinois and two other states in the next year and a half, it is over for women in this century."[6]

Members voted to extend officer and board terms by one year in order to provide continuity during this critical period and to allow full concentration on the ERA drive. In the final years of the drive approximately one-quarter of NOW's entire budget was devoted to the ERA. In the revised 1980 budget 24 percent of total expenditures were earmarked for the ERA versus 6.75 percent for general action programs.[7] In 1981 25 percent of total expenditures were allocated for the ERA campaign and 9 percent for all other issues.[8]

As the deadline for ratification approached, the campaign lost its identification with roots in first-wave feminism as anti-ERA groups increasingly painted the amendment as a radical proposal. As Jane Mansbridge shows, ERA activists tended to argue that ratification would bring about much more dramatic changes for women than its passage would likely have achieved.[9] Throughout the ratification campaign the courts began applying the Fourteenth Amendment's equal protection clause to sex discrimination, for example. Ironically, although the radicalization of the amendment helped seal its fate, it is also what drove thousands of NOW members (in addition to the members of other organizations) to contribute time and money to the cause—in some cases abandoning jobs and their home states for the duration.

Mansbridge argues that the failure of the ERA campaign can be explained in large part by the fact that volunteers, rather than paid staff, played significant roles. These findings apply to any organization trying to secure public goods with volunteers. Members of social movement groups require incentives to devote resources to a public cause; because ERA campaigners wanted to feel that their work on ratification mattered, they exaggerated its likely impact. Volunteers are notoriously difficult to fire; they demand more autonomy than paid staff, making it difficult for leaders to stifle, for example, local chapters' tactical choices even when such plans risk raising the ire of the very political targets activists hope to influence.[10] As one news report said, "The women leaders who embraced lesbian rights, who spat at state capitol policemen, who did not understand how to win political allies . . . could not be taken seriously."[11]

The exigencies of maintaining the loyalty of unpaid activists constrained the ability of leaders of the ERA fight to conduct the most politically palatable and expedient campaign. As Mansbridge shows, however, volunteer-based organizations working on behalf of the ERA differed with respect to the appropriate way to depict the effects of its ratification and regarding the tactics to employ. How do we explain such differences in apparently similar organizations?

It is not just that NOW leaders lacked the bureaucratic means to control activists. In joining NOW, members also became participants in a political system. By attending meetings, reading newsletters, communicating with other activists, and comparing NOW values and practices with those of other organizations, NOW members developed expectations about what issues and tactics the group should pursue. For their part, NOW leaders rose in the organization as a result of their demonstrated belief in and adherence to the group's principles and practices. NOW's decision-making processes further linked leaders to members through regular and competitive local and national elections.

The Rising Power of Conservatives

During Carter's presidency the National Organization for Women (along with many other liberal organizations, including the NAACP, the United Farm Workers, and labor unions such as the UAW) felt itself "on a collision course with the Democratic Party."[12] Carter's firing of Bella Abzug, longtime NOW supporter and president and cofounder of the National Women's Political Caucus, from his Advisory Council for Women in 1978 set the tone for his administration's attitude toward women's rights. Many Abzug supporters left the council in protest, and the reformulated group had "clearly" changed: "It looks like a pink ribbon committee, with no political or economic clout, no strong ties with industry. It is instead dominated by people representing religious women's groups, ethnic women's organizations, and such traditional groups as the Future Homemakers and the American Association of University Women."[13]

The rising political influence of the right within the Republican Party also increasingly galled NOW activists. In 1979 Reverend Jerry Falwell formed his nationally successful conservative organization the "Moral Majority," which endorsed Ronald Reagan's presidential candidacy and by 1980 boasted two million members.[14] The Life Amendment Political Action Committee (LAPAC); the National Conservative Political Action Committee (NCPAC), created in 1974; and Paul Weyrich's Committee for the Survival of a Free Congress all invested heavily in electoral politics.[15] In 1980 President Smeal declared to members that the most critical battles were those being waged in the electoral arena: "We are in the midst of the 1980 election campaigns with a resurging Far Right determined to defeat pro–women's rights candidates and to return women and the nation to the last century. The battle is being fought in selected legislative and Congressional campaigns throughout the nation. NOW/PACs, but most importantly, feminists, are everywhere fighting the—at last—visible political opposition to women's rights."[16]

The election of President Reagan in 1980 confirmed the political ascendance of the New Right and the Religious Right.[17] Responding to changing political circumstances, at its 1980 national conference

NOW rescinded an earlier resolution opposing President Carter's re-election, stating that the Republican Party "is now held totally captive by the Radical Right" and "is being used by the Radical Right to change the face of America by . . . using the millions of dollars big business is pouring into political action committees, to seize control of state legislatures and control of the Congress of the United States itself; . . . In light of these dire developments NOW cannot remain on the sidelines."[18] The 1980 conference delegates voted to mobilize against Reagan's election, to expose his viewpoints to the American people, and to "launch an unceasing campaign to turn out votes for our friends in Congress and in the state legislatures."[19]

The activities of citizen groups specifically targeting the feminist agenda also colored feminists' assessments of the sociopolitical environment of the early 1980s. Anti-ERA organizations such as Phyllis Schlafly's STOP-ERA, for example, effectively portrayed NOW and feminist movement groups as extremists intent on destroying the American family. In their campaign against the goals of groups such as NOW, antifeminists had found an important ally in the new presidential administration: "The Reagan administration looked benignly on a right-wing counterattack against the modest feminist legislative gains and organizational funding. As women's organizations faced conservative backlash in the 1980s, the distinction between 'radical' and 'mainstream' feminism continued to fade. Even the most mainstream feminist issues, such as educational equity, came under attack."[20]

In this atmosphere abortion rights revived as a critical issue for feminists.[21] Abortion-rights opponents gained in power and visibility, some forming groups to target the clinics where women managed their reproductive health and received abortions. The *Washington Post* documented the rising level of anti-abortion activism: "Staging sit-ins at abortion clinics and sending 'truth teams' to try to persuade prospective abortion patients that they should not abort their pregnancies, the antiabortion protesters have kept alive an issue that many thought was settled with the Supreme Court's 1973 ruling legalizing most abortions." A NOW official responded, "They're getting stronger and more sophisticated. It's really scary, we're definitely worried about it."[22] The conservative political environment precipitated membership increases in some feminist and liberal organizations, including NOW: according to Karen Mulhauser, leader of NARAL, membership in that organization grew from almost nine thousand in 1977 to sixty thousand in January 1979.[23]

After Reagan, a staunch opponent of abortion, took office, NOW noted an increase in violent acts perpetrated against women's health clinics and the doctors and employees who worked in them.[24] The reintroduction of the Human Life Amendment (HLA) in Congress, a bill that exposed physicians to prosecution if they provided abortions, was a further inducement for pro-choice activists. The *National NOW Times* said,

> President Reagan is orchestrating the assault [on abortion rights] on all fronts from the White House—by his appointment of well-known anti-abortion and anti–birth control leaders to top positions in the Department of Health and Human Services; by his administration's regulations and proposals that make it more difficult to get an abortion and to use preferred methods of birth control; and by his endorsement of a constitutional amendment that would prohibit abortion and certain forms of birth control.[25]

Such threats to the 1973 *Roe v. Wade* decision convinced many feminists that the judiciary could not be relied on to uphold feminist gains, a position underscored by the appointment of conservative judges throughout the 1980s. At the same time, the rescission battles initiated by anti-ERA activists forced NOW to wage in state courts (to prevent states from rescinding their ratification of the ERA) further testified to the fact that feminists required stronger and more reliable allies within state legislatures. In fact, even appointments of women to federal office fell during Reagan's tenure, further depleting the pool of possible feminist allies. Representative Patricia Schroeder (D-Colo.), chair of the Subcommittee on Civil Service of the House Committee on Post Office and Civil Service, found that by midterm, Carter's appointments of women (22.4%) greatly exceeded that of Reagan (14.6%).[26]

Political Activity

NOW's burgeoning presence in the electoral arena during this period reflected a general trend among women's rights activists. Feminist organizations became progressively more involved in identifying winnable seats for women in party politics and in financing political campaigns.[27] Whereas in 1974 only one women's political action committee existed, by July 1983 there were sixteen.[28] Prior to 1977 NOW had no political action committee; five years later it boasted eighty-one PACs in forty states.[29]

The discovery of a "gender gap" (a term Ellie Smeal claims to have coined) in the 1980 elections encouraged NOW leaders who immediately reported the phenomenon to its members, to policymakers, and electoral candidates.[30] One UPI writer noted that "Republicans are so worried about the women's vote in the 1982 congressional elections that their campaign manual urges candidates to play up their identification with women's groups wherever possible."[31] Indeed, as the ERA campaign heated up in the 1980s, a common chant heard at marches and rallies was "We Will Remember in November."

Electoral Politics

Although opinion polls seemed to demonstrate the public's endorsement of many feminist goals, similar levels of support were not forthcoming from legislators. Marches, rallies, and public outreach all drew enthusiastic crowds, but these efforts did not result in ERA victories in state legislatures. NOW leaders argued that activists were therefore forced to participate in electoral politics.[32]

In 1979 NOW created guidelines for handling political endorsements within the organization. In addition, in December 1979 "the NOW national board . . . voted unanimously to recommend to the NOW Political Action Committee (NOW/PAC) that it opposes the nomination and re-election of President Jimmy Carter. The recommendation was unanimously passed by the PAC the same weekend."[33] Later that year the national board voted to recommend to the NOW/PAC that it endorse Kennedy as the Democratic presidential nominee and Anderson as the Republican. NOW's decision to reject President Carter, brought about by his failure to lend adequate support for ERA ratification and Medicaid funding for abortions, was entirely in keeping with the organization's promise to maintain its political independence.[34] Yet, the decision irked some NOW members, other feminist organizations such as the NWPC and National Abortion Rights Action League (NARAL), and other liberal groups who preferred Carter to more conservative alternatives.[35]

Organizations such as the bipartisan National Women's Political Caucus and the Republican Women's Campaign Fund began enjoying great success in fund-raising on behalf of electoral candidates supportive of the ERA. "We have just had money pouring in," said one NWPC representative, having "raised more than $325,000 for support of more than 100 candidates."[36]

NOW's annual conference delegates voted to urge members to pressure politicians at the Democratic and Republican conventions. State and national NOW leaders kept members and one another apprised as to proposed delegate rules; national and state organizations placed action teams on alert during primaries and compiled state delegate selection information. This valuable information, together with the guidance offered at "how to" workshops at conferences, paved the way for NOW members to run as delegates to the national party conventions.

Party Politics

The intricacies of party politics became increasingly transparent to the group as larger numbers of NOW's members and leaders worked to influence the Democratic and Republican parties from the inside. NOW Vice President Jane Wells-Schooley, President Eleanor Smeal, and NOW activist Molly Yard were active in party politics. Wells-Schooley, for example, testified on the inclusion of women's rights issues before the Democratic Party's temporary platform committee in 1980, and Molly Yard, a member of the Rules Committee, also served as floor manager for the provision (Article 11), which provided for the equal representation of women at all levels of Democratic Party organization.[37] NOW members comprised more than two hundred of the delegates and alternates to the 1980 Democratic convention.[38] In 1978 "the Democratic Party approved a rule change . . . requiring that 50 percent of the 3,331 delegates to its 1980 convention be women."[39] Feminist gains resulting from the parity achieved at the convention exemplified the benefits of seeking equal political representation.[40] "As the Democratic Party development and platform have been changed by equal division of delegates, so can the Congress and the state legislatures of this country be changed in equal division. . . . Until we have women legislators in numbers equal to men our issues will continue to receive short shrift. . . . Therefore . . . the National Organization for Women calls for and commits itself to work for parity in the legislative halls of this nation and at every level of government."[41] In addition, as women gained proportionate representation in parties and legislatures the risk that feminist organizations would feel pressure to compromise their political independence by aligning with one party or another, lessened. Nor would they be tempted to moderate their goals. The equal representation of women at the 1980 convention, for example, furnished feminists with the numerical power to resist policy compromise and the co-optation of their positions.[42]

The Republican Party reversed its historic commitment to the ERA in 1980; that year the Democratic Party supported its passage for the first time. This reversal did not cause NOW to abandon hope of influencing Republicans, nor did the group intend to align itself with Democrats. In fact, disgusted by the parties' lackluster performance on women's issues, NOW resolved to organize protests at both 1980 national conventions.

Prevailing despite the opposition of President Carter's delegates to the Democratic conventions, feminists won the adoption of one plank in the platform that enjoined the party from providing assistance to candidates who failed to endorse the ERA and another that called for federal funding of abortions for Medicaid patients.[43] In addition to enacting equal gender representation in its delegations, "the Rules Committee had voted to amend the Democratic Party

Charter to provide equal division . . . also on the membership of the Democratic National Committee, the Executive Committee, all national official Party bodies, and state central committees."[44] Though NOW continued to emphasize its nonpartisanship, feminist lobbying consistently failed to make similar gains within the Republican Party.

Upholding Guiding Principles and Practices

As the ERA campaign evolved, it shed its reputation as a mainstream project, lessening some members' hesitations about NOW's commitment to it. For example, NOW emphasized the dramatic impact of ratification when group leaders affirmed in 1980, at a critical stage in the ERA campaign, that the ERA would—and should—require women's inclusion in the military draft.[45]

Bolstering anti-ERA groups' arguments about NOW's radical agenda, NOW's argument that the ERA applied the military draft to women proved enormously costly for the ERA movement. Despite organizing activities such as its 1980 "Family Day for the ERA" rally on the steps of Houston's City Hall, NOW's position on women and the draft hampered its ability to claim that it represented the views and interests of the average woman or the average voter.

Some NOW activists (whose number had grown dramatically as a result of the ERA campaign) balked at the radical notion of sending women into combat. Yet others were more concerned that NOW would follow its compatriots in the ERA fight who were downplaying the measure's potential to effect significant social, political, and economic change. Member trepidation heightened once the ratification deadline was extended, as the coalition of groups working for the passage of the ERA began pressing for a "new moderation," as the *Washington Post* noted: "A subtle shift has occurred in the long fight. . . . Backers are desperately trying to make the amendment an establishment issue . . . casting themselves as middle of the roaders. Militant feminists are being told to lower their voices and profiles.

The tactical emphasis is on electioneering and hardball politics, not emotion."[46]

One way NOW members and leaders remained faithful to the organization's principles was by continuing to address issues other than the ERA. For example, though activists attending the 1978 conference rebuffed one faction's attempt to abandon the ratification drive, they did unanimously approve a measure directing members and leaders to "defeat legislative efforts that would restrict the rights of homosexuals." Other conference resolutions reveal activists' sensitivity to the need to integrate electoral tactics with grassroots participation and empowerment. In 1981, when conference participants authorized the use of electoral tactics on behalf of reproductive rights, they also declared that, "the election strategy [will] be centered around maximum involvement of NOW members in recruiting of candidates and the development of campaign support through the training of campaign staff and volunteers."[47]

NOW leaders combined political campaigning with other tactics. For example, the group began its "ERA Emergency" project by threatening economic boycotts of fifteen unratified states. The move attracted the support of other liberal groups as well as labor organizations such as the AFL-CIO. Following the recommendation of the Coalition of Trade Union Women in 1979, the AFL-CIO decided not to hold its annual conference in Florida.[48] In response to critics of such a move, Alice Cohan, then field adviser of the national NOW ERA Strike Force, said, "The reality is that we're playing hard-ball. To say it's not nice [to threaten election defeat and economic boycotts] is not to understand the electoral system in this country . . . a tea boycott started the American revolution."[49]

As the original 1979 deadline for ratification loomed, NOW and several hundred other groups organized a nationwide demonstration to "rescue the ERA" and lobby for a seven-year extension.[50] NOW also conducted vigils in front of the White House (including one thirty-seven-day fast by eight members), door-to-door education campaigns, walkathons, marches dedicated to the memory of suffragists, and protests at Mormon temples (one of which involved activists chaining themselves to temple gates) and conservative churches. And when voting to pursue the ERA and other goals through more conventional methods, members acknowledged the group's investment in maintaining a diverse tactical repertoire. When members resolved to commit NOW to raise $10 million toward a major ERA media campaign, the measure stated that, "women of this nation deserve the most modern and comprehensive campaign possible in pursuit of their justice; [and] a several state media campaign is an essential part of a successful contemporary national political campaign. . . . We reaffirm the multi-tactical, comprehensive nature of the national ERA Countdown Media Campaign which employs political and legislative pressure, mass organizing, grassroots lobbying, coalition building."[51] National conference workshops (most frequently organized for members by leaders) consistently covered a wide array of issues and tactics, including worksite organizing, mental health initiatives, early childhood development, the organization of homemakers, feminist consciousness-raising, insurance and credit discrimination, and women in the military.

Smeal's leadership ability, together with her willingness to make the adoption of the ERA a top priority and to venture into political campaigning frequently engendered complaints. Some members groused that her leadership threatened the integrity of NOW's governance structure. When she ran unopposed in 1980 for a second term, the *Washington Post* remarked on Smeal's organizational skills and iron will: "Her administrative machine rolled all over challengers at the NOW convention. . . . And she is tough: she dumped two of her first-term officers and demanded that their supporters accept it."[52] (One reporter observed that Phyllis Schlafly and Ellie Smeal both wielded "viselike grips" on their organizations.)[53] Yet, among Smeal's carefully chosen officers were activists such as Arlie Scott, vice president for action programs and a lesbian, who declared that, "I don't want NOW to be another broad civil rights organization. . . . I want it to be purely feminist."[54]

Under Smeal's guidance, NOW continued to take vanguard political stands. Lesbian activists helped maintain NOW's commitments in this regard. They were "a strong voice within NOW, trying continually to make the organization even more the cutting edge of feminism than it is," according to the *Washington Post*.[55] At NOW's 1980 conference the *Post* reported:

> Workshop sessions on lesbian rights, which NOW has long en-
> dorsed . . . were among the most heavily attended and emotional of
> the conference. Nearly a dozen competing resolutions on the subject
> were among more than 150 introduced for conference debate.' The
> one that passed set up a campaign for enactment of comprehensive
> gay and lesbian rights legislation at the state, federal and municipal
> levels. A section supporting gays "as long as their activities . . . do not
> violate NOW policies" was deleted after being called an insult.[56]

Shortly after the meeting Smeal spoke at a gay rights demonstration that included representatives from the National Gay Task Force and the Lesbian Feminism Liberation groups.

Working with such other organizations as the Coalition of Labor Union Women, the ACLU, and Planned Parenthood, NOW pressed for Medicaid funding for poor women who wanted abortions; along with others (in a coalition ultimately called Save Our Security), NOW worked to stop President Carter's proposed reductions in So-cial Security benefits.[57] In response to the passage in 1979 of the Hyde Amendment, which eliminated financial assistance for indigent women seeking abortions, NOW's New York City chapter held a "teach-in" at media outlets.[58]

Also in coalition, NOW petitioned the FCC to block the sale of television stations whose owners, they claimed, failed to actively re-cruit minority stakeholders or to hire minorities and women in broadcasting.[59] NOW member Peg Wallace testified before Congress in support of decriminalizing prostitution.[60] NOW leaders fought alongside the NAACP and other groups to bring antitrust suits against the insurance industry, which, they alleged, denied minori-ties, women, and the poor the policies necessary for them to acquire real property.[61] The group printed and distributed information for battered women and displaced homemakers and supported office workers' strikes.[62] NOW also formed part of a coalition (in a con-ference organized by the Women's International League for Peace and Freedom) that met with the State Department and the U.S. Arms Control and Disarmament Agency to lobby on behalf of nuclear disarmament.[63]

NOW Board Resolutions, 1969–1983

Political conditions increasingly favored NOW's rising commitment to the issue of the ERA and to the tactic of electoral activism throughout the late 1970s and early 1980s. The potential benefits of this strategy were many, including the issue's ability to attract numerous new members. The risks of abstaining from the ERA drive or from joining the electoral fray on its behalf, on the other hand, appeared high, especially as the Reagan administration came to power. Yet as we have seen, NOW's embrace of the ratification campaign and of the tactics used in its pursuit did not occur without significant internal debate.

An analysis of all national board meeting resolutions between the years 1969 and 1983 confirms that electoral activism did not overtake other issues on national NOW's agenda, though this was one of the main reservations activists expressed.[64]

Over time the proportion of resolutions devoted to NOW's basic organizational maintenance increased steadily and significantly, from a low of 4.94 percent in 1969 to 83.45 percent in 1983. Member benefits or outreach-related activity, a subcategory of organizational maintenance resolutions, shows peaks in 1973 (17.42 percent) and 1982 (21.05 percent) but otherwise hovers between 6 and 9 percent throughout most of the period.

No clear pattern exists for electoral activity throughout this period except that after 1974 at least one resolution was passed every year on electoral activity—never again zero, as occasionally occurred before 1975. At their peak, board resolutions relating to electoral activity represented a little over 4 percent of resolutions in 1979 but in general remained under (sometimes well under) 3 percent of total resolutions passed in each year since then.

To hone in more closely on the question of NOW's participation

TABLE 5.1.
Motions at NOW National Board Meetings

Category of Motions	Examples
Organizational maintenance activities	Budget, procedure, staffing, membership
Member benefits	Training, insurance benefits, publications, retreats
Influence acitvities	Take a position, declare state of emergency, finance activity
External relations	Form coalitions, act as consultants, media relations
Protest/Grassroots activities	Marches, walkathon, petition, refusal to pay taxes
Legislative/Lobbying activities	Testify, recommend appointments, lobby Congress
Legal Activities	Join lawsuit, file formal complaint, demand compliance with federal law
Electoral Activities	Recruit candidates, influence political platforms, contribute financial aid

in electoral activism, I divided the data into two periods, the first spanning the years 1969 to 1975 and the second the years 1976 to 1983. In 1975, for the first time, the question of the legitimacy of the electoral strategy took center stage in NOW's national elections. Delegates elected a grassroots-oriented president, Karen DeCrow, but they also chose a national board that favored political action. Dividing the data in this fashion allows us to analyze the enduring effects of these controversies.

When we compare the average percentage of resolutions passed in each category of activity in the two time periods, two categories of initiatives besides that of organizational maintenance increased in the second period: member benefits and electoral politics, though the latter enjoyed only an extremely modest boost. In fact, the most important trend in this data is the much greater prominence of general organizational maintenance activity during the period 1976–83; whereas over 80 percent of initiatives in the earlier period involved some form of activism, only 40 percent of initiatives did so in the latter period.

In short, institutionalized forms of activism did not crowd out protest politics at the NOW board meetings. Instead, this task may have been accomplished, at least on the national level, by NOW's bureaucratic concerns. I find no general contraction in NOW's tactical repertoire (for example, activities focusing on the support of electoral campaigns do not overshadow activities involving grassroots mobilization). In addition, resolutions concerning outreach to members increased during this period.

Preparing Members for Failure and a New Strategy

Well before the ratification deadline arrived in mid-1982, NOW's leaders began preparing members for the possibility of the ERA's failure. As the *National NOW Times* reported, at NOW's annual conference in 1980, President Smeal did not pretend success was inevitable:

> I cannot, will not promise victory. I'm begging you and begging us not to save this organization for something else, but to put it on the line now for equality. There is something wrong when we must be assured a victory. We must be willing to put ourselves on the line for the principle of equality for women. . . . Knowing that all the political pundits will tell us that we will lose. Knowing that they are probably right under normal circumstances. But knowing that it is our duty, responsibility, love, commitment to women's equality. And knowing that our belief that it can be done is as important as all the wisdom of those political analysts.[65]

Smeal warned legislators in 1982 about the new electoral threat NOW posed: "If [legislators] cynically thwart women's just and reasonable demands for equal rights under the law, they will discover a new reality on July 1. Not only will our determination be undiminished, but our numbers and our political skills will be vastly increased."[66] As a Republican sponsor of a ratification attempt that failed in 1980 in Illinois (despite an extraordinary mobilization on its behalf) said, "If you can't change the minds, change the bodies."[67] The battle in Illinois to overturn the rule that required a three-fifths majority to ratify the amendment illustrated the importance of having allies inside legislative institutions. Illinois House Speaker

George Ryan proved the major obstacle in this fight in his refusal to allow consideration of a change.

Smeal's reaction was shaped by the dissonance between the apparent public support for the ERA and the failure to secure its ratification in Illinois and in states such as North Carolina.[68] Just before the ratification deadline, for example, a Harris Survey found that public support for the amendment reached 63 percent nationwide.[69] North Carolinians voiced similar levels of support. However, as the *National NOW Times* reported, "despite the fact that North Carolinians favored the ERA by a 60–31% margin, the Senate voted to table the Amendment, 27–23. In fact, opponent senators showed an overwhelming disregard for the wishes of their constituents. According to polls taken in 12 districts represented by 17 senators, public support ranged from a high of 65% for ERA . . . to a low of 56% [in favor]."[70]

When President Smeal ended NOW's efforts to ratify the ERA on June 24, 1982, NOW's primary organizational challenge was to maintain the resources gained during the campaign. To stave off disillusionment within its ranks of activists and donors, NOW's leadership needed to explain the failure in terms that shifted the focus of attention to a new battle.

Smeal outlined the obstacles encountered on the ratification drive and the major reasons it failed. She emphasized in particular NOW's inability to marshal the support of either legislators or the public by lobbying. Feminists, Smeal argued, must become legislators themselves. The reasons for the ERA's demise, she argued, included (1) the new Republican opposition to women's rights, (2) the lukewarm support of Democrats for the ERA, (3) the opposition of "special corporate interests" such as insurance companies, which contributed to anti-ERA groups and legislators directly, and (4) "sex bias" in the legislatures.[71]

Smeal focused not only on the concerted Republican opposition to the ERA but also the reluctance of Democrats to lend their full support to secure its passage. Just a few days after she formally ended NOW's ERA campaign, the group held a rally in Philadelphia to impress on Democrats "that although women are showing a preference for Democrats in the polls, the Democrats can't take women for granted. . . . If the Democrats will not discipline their party membership, we will. Women's support . . . will not be automatically granted. . . . The women's movement is an independent political force."[72]

When its struggle for the ERA ended, NOW found itself flush not only with money and members but also with political contacts and valuable information about electoral campaign cycles and the inner workings of both state and federal legislatures. The *National NOW Times* noted: "The decade long battle for ERA has been a political training ground for women. Even if they lose the war, they have learned well how to play the game. The troops in the National Organization for Women and sister groups who have fought for ERA now know how to lobby legislators, run candidates for office, hold news conferences, raise money, stage rallies, and effectively use both the news media and paid advertising to get their message across."[73] NOW's members also gained an enormous amount of experience in creative and cutting-edge techniques of fund-raising.[74] By 1982 the organization proved capable of raising $1 million per month via direct mail.[75] NOW's sophistication in terms of lobbying tactics, the organization and management of rallies and protests, and understanding the kinds of influence it could wield in electoral contests had grown dramatically.

NOW wove together its explanation for the loss of ERA (and other setbacks, such as the Supreme Court's 1980 ruling that allowed the withholding of Medicaid funding for abortion procedures) with a new strategic vision. The new plan refocused members' anger about the ERA loss toward a battleground, the electoral arena, where the lessons leaders and members acquired during the ERA fight could be used.

NOW's success in Florida's elections immediately following the end of the ERA drive suggested the great potential in embarking on an electorally focused strategy. In August 1982 the *National NOW Times* reported a strong increase in the numbers of women filing as candidates in Florida state legislative races after the defeat of the ERA there in June. Smeal noted: "This development is a dramatic indication that we are entering a new era of direct political participation for women. . . . We are committed to working to increase the numbers of women holding elected office, to support those who supported women's rights issues, and to remove from office as many opponents as possible."[76] NOW member, officer, and future president Patricia Ireland called this change

> a significant shift in NOW's strategy—what then-President Ellie Smeal called a "feminization of power." Instead of just trying to influence those in power, we would now become the people in power. . . . In the six weeks between the defeat of the ERA and the filing deadline for the 1982 elections in Florida, we conducted an urgent search to convince strong feminist women to run for political office. . . . Our strategy worked. Not only did we get more women elected, but we also inspired new campaign workers and women voters by having candidates in whom we could believe with our whole hearts.[77]

The end of the ratification drive for the ERA coincided with new elections for NOW officers. Smeal stepped down as president, but her successor, Judy Goldsmith (who had been an officer during Smeal's term), also pledged to continue strengthening and expanding NOW's political power. At a news conference in 1982 Goldsmith asserted: "I see the [NOW election] results as a strong mandate for the continuation of the electoral political direction we've taken for the last year. . . . Our organization stands for full participation of women in every area and that means in politics. . . . We are strengthening our political action committees and putting strong emphasis on the economic issues relevant to women."[78]

NOW's emphasis on the importance of electoral politics to feminists as the ERA drive wound down provoked renewed debates about its efficacy and legitimacy. NOW's involvement in electoral activism during the ERA campaign had met with mixed results; not all members were convinced of the superiority of electoral activism, since it appeared difficult to ensure a legislator's loyalty once the election ended.[79] In addition, activists imagined that NOW's organizational unity would suffer as a result of partisan battles. During the Carter administration, members worried about alienating Democrats; now members predicted that Republican members would feel like outcasts. The *National NOW Times* reported that, "much of the current Republican political leadership is opposed to the Equal Rights Amendment. . . . ERA proponents can no longer ignore the demonstrated opposition of the Republican political leadership to the Equal Rights Amendment and to women's rights. The issue is rapidly becoming, despite the efforts of Republicans who believe in individual rights, a partisan issue."[80] As the National Organization for Women embarked on another decade of organizing, culminating in what the media dubbed the "Year of the Woman" in electoral politics in 1992 (a phrase the media had also used to describe 1972 and 1984), the group continued to grapple with dilemmas related to the political system established by activists more than twenty years earlier.

6. From the ERA Strategy to the Electoral Strategy

We learned an important lesson: All the grassroots
work in the world won't result in progress if there
aren't enough women . . . elected.

Patricia Ireland

The worst thing we can do right now is try to become acceptable.

Eleanor Cutri Smeal

Even with the overwhelming support of the public, the mobilization of tens of thousands of activists, and the support of Congress, the Equal Rights Amendment failed to be ratified by three-quarters of state legislatures by 1982. The decade between the close of the ERA campaign and the presidential election of Democrat William Jefferson Clinton in 1992 presented NOW with three critical challenges.

The first crisis NOW faced in the post-ERA period was the task of shifting the organization and its members from the massive investment and mobilization for the ERA to new issues and tactics. NOW's membership ranks and finances had swelled enormously during the ERA drive; the loss of this mobilizing issue thus posed a critical problem. In 1982 NOW's membership rolls listed approximately 220,000 contributing members, but over the next few years the organization's membership plummeted by about 90,000.[1] The second involved a crisis of leadership and finances in 1985 that nearly destroyed the group. The political prominence of the New Right and the concomitant threat posed by its activists and sympathetic legislators to abortion rights constituted the third major challenge.

Each of these crises brought to the foreground questions about organizational strategy. According to Roberta Spalter-Roth and Ronnee Schreiber, the feminist organizations that successfully navigated the hostile political environment of the 1980s were those that managed to overcome internal group conflicts over strategy choice and change. A major source of disagreement involving questions about the legitimacy of becoming involved in partisan politics arose in many feminist organizations, including the National Women's Political Caucus.[2] Some groups, among them the Women's Equity Action League (WEAL) and the Project on Equal Education Rights (PEER), had difficulty maintaining the loyalty of activists and the vitality of their organizations as they increased their participation in mainstream forms of political action in the 1980s. All feminist organizations, Spalter-Roth and Schreiber note, "faced charges that they were irrelevant to most women, were outdated survivors of a more radical era, and had been co-opted and could no longer stir or mobilize the marching millions": "First, there was tension between marketing feminist issues in the dominant language of individual liberalism, while simultaneously trying to raise collective consciousness, to mobilize, and to educate around structural issues. . . . [In addition], tension arose between claims to speak for all women and the limited success achieved in trying to recruit a more diverse membership, to participate in diverse coalitions, and to put issues of importance to women of color, lesbians, and working-class women on the policy agenda."[3]

Jo Freeman, the first political scientist to examine the National Organization for Women in depth, viewed NOW's involvement in party politics during this decade with similar skepticism. Freeman argued that social movement organizations that participate in electoral politics risk such adverse consequences as co-optation and the exodus of these groups' "radical flank." In her view, a social movement organization cannot be both a radical advocate of social change and a significant player in the institutionalized political arena. In the case of NOW, "the Democratic Party's traditional approach to insurgent groups is to co-opt them. The price of becoming an insider is that one must abide by the inevitable requirement to curtail one's commitment to one's own agenda. . . . NOW may . . . decide to [do so] but the consequence . . . will be to remove it from the cutting edge of social change. . . . Since an organization cannot be both in the mainstream and in the radical flank without losing credibility and legitimacy, NOW will have to choose which path to follow."[4]

Managing the End of the ERA Campaign: Launching the Electoral Strategy

NOW's first crisis, handling the demise of the ERA, left the group with two fundamental challenges critical to its long-term stability and viability. One of these challenges was to maintain the political and economic resources it had gained during the ten-year ERA campaign. President Smeal underscored how the ERA ratification drive transformed the group:

> We have developed a network of 750 phone banks which have worked and will continue to work for women's rights, a funding base which is bringing in more money monthly than the Democratic Party, an experienced nationwide volunteer and professional corps which numbers in the thousands, and an award-winning media advertising program. The campaign also generated such widespread, enthusiastic support that it has been able to continually produce mass public events, ranging from such single-site events as the ERA Extension March in 1978 that brought 100,000 people to Washington, D.C., to the simultaneous rallies of more than 10,000 each in four unratified state capitols on June 6.[5]

Anticipating a dip in its membership rolls, NOW embarked on a membership drive shortly after June 1982, taking advantage of the group's publicity. NOW also committed to renew its investment in a broad range of feminist issues while retaining the passage of the

ERA as one of its priorities. In December 1982 board members also increased funds for chapter development to help integrate former ERA volunteers further into the organization and to encourage new membership.[6]

NOW's presidents during this decade—Judy Goldsmith (1982–85), Eleanor Smeal (1985–87), Molly Yard (1987–91), and Patricia Ireland (1991–2001)—agreed on the value of the strategy change. Conceptually, these leaders framed the electoral strategy in radical terms, as a means of attacking the establishment. Practically speaking, they linked the implementation of the strategy to NOW's governance structure by organizing grassroots workshops on electoral political action and launching a voter registration drive.[7]

Of course, electoral politics was not a new tactic for the organization, but NOW leaders were now arguing that electoral participation was not only a tactic (a means to achieve legislative goals by helping elect feminist politicians) but an end in itself. The gender gap in voting, NOW leaders said, showed that women and men held significantly different positions on many issues. Women lacked legislative representation of their political views, and this inequality could be corrected only by establishing an ongoing feminist presence in electoral politics.

Outgoing president Smeal pointed out the token representation of women in the unratified states of North Carolina, Illinois, Oklahoma, and Florida. In these legislatures the ERA was supported by 75 percent of women lawmakers in contrast to 46 percent of the men.[8] Smeal's claims were borne out more generally in a 1981 study by the Center for American Women and Politics (CAWP), reported in the *National NOW Times*, which surveyed elected officials on their positions on the ERA. In 1982 women constituted only 6 percent of candidates for congressional and no more than 20 percent of candidates for state legislative elections.[9] Smeal argued:

> Unquestionably, the most significant and historic outcome of this campaign is that it will usher in a new era of direct political participation for women. Untold thousands of women have lobbied legislators in the course of this campaign, and what many of them discovered,

time and time again, was that they were better qualified to hold office than the men they were lobbying. . . . We are determined to seek direct and just representation for women in government; we are determined to build an independent political force, with the freedom and flexibility to support candidates or not support candidates based upon their proven commitments to women's rights. . . . NOW seeks to recruit and elect a new breed of candidate.[10]

For NOW, this "new breed" of candidate need not be female, only feminist. NOW leaders placed the blame for the failure of the ERA squarely on the shoulders of legislators who had "betrayed" them. These legislators' broken promises to the movement, maintained NOW leaders, demonstrated that feminists could no longer depend on the empty assurances of representatives: instead, they must enter the halls of power themselves. NOW leaders thus constructed a "causal story" that showed that the organization must focus more heavily on electoral activism.

Smeal also vowed that NOW would expand the use of economic boycotts and "media educational campaigns" to attack companies profiting from discrimination against women. The passage of the ERA would not be abandoned as a goal, she said, but activists would have to work to change the political climate to secure a reasonable chance of its success. Patricia Ireland, NOW president from 1991 to 2001, noted in her memoirs that it was clear to the leadership why the ERA had failed: "We had to get more women and people of color into elected office. Period."[11] She also asserted, "When state legislators failed to ratify the ERA in 1982, we learned an important lesson: All the grassroots work in the world won't result in progress if there aren't enough women . . . elected."[12]

Immediately following the close of the ERA ratification campaign NOW redeployed the activists who had been working on its passage in North Carolina to work in that state's electoral primaries, targeting the campaigns of those who had voted against the amendment. NOW's newsletter reported on their efforts: "A core of Countdown Campaign activists demonstrated their organizational ability by putting together all the nuts and bolts of the [North Carolina] cam-

paign, including phone banking, mailing and literature drops. . . .
Their effort continues to point up the development of feminism as a
third force in American politics."[13]

NOW, along with other women's groups, also vowed to increase
the financial resources of feminist candidates. In September 1982 the
group reported, "NOW PACs pledge that at least 20% of all
fundraising will be set aside for recruiting and training candidates,
campaign managers, and workers for future races. NOW/PACs will
create an institute for women's policies to help develop a new breed
of political candidate committed to women's rights."[14] In December
the board recommended that a line item in the NOW/Equality/PAC
budget be established to train feminist electoral candidates. NOW
also made a point of supporting its own activists in their political
forays, voting to set aside $50,000 for them.[15]

Urging members to capitalize on the skills gained during the ERA
mobilization, NOW leaders organized workshops like the one held
at the 1983 annual conference called "We'll Remember Each November!" Activists attending the meeting were told that "during the
ERA and other women's rights campaigns, NOW has learned political skills that are directly transferable to election campaigns." Workshops like this one addressed such issues as "campaign management
and policy development in a candidate's campaign; converting issue
phone banks to political phone banks; [and] models of individual
chapter, state and national NOW involvement in specific campaigns."[16]

The tactic of organizing ERA walkathons proved such a valuable
source of income for NOW that in April 1982 the national board
voted that these events should henceforth be organized to subsidize
its political action committees.[17] In August NOW held a
PAC/Woman Walk to raise money for its state-level PACs.[18] Since
their legal establishment in the early 1970s, the number of political
action committees representing an astounding variety of interests
had risen dramatically.[19] Committees supporting women's and feminists' campaigns experienced similar increases. In 1984 approximately twenty women's PACs existed around the country; the three
largest were those of the Women's Campaign Fund, the National Or-

ganization for Women, and the National Women's Political Caucus.[20] In 1985 a new women's PAC formed: "EMILY's List," whose name stands for "Early Money Is Like Yeast: It Makes the Dough Rise." In other words, campaigns that are successful in fund-raising early attract more support. EMILY's List quickly became the most successful feminist political action committee.

The Gender Gap

The NOW national conference of 1982 was the first to hold workshops geared to exploit the apparent gender gap within the electorate. As NWPC leader Alice Travis affirmed, "Women . . . make up 60 percent of the registered Democrats and they outvoted men in both parties by four million in 1982. They are a force."[21]

Responding to these gender differences in voting behavior, in 1984 the Democratic Party launched a voter registration drive aimed at women and hired Ellie Smeal (after she stepped down as NOW's president in 1982) as a political consultant; she produced a "party handbook" titled "Maximizing the Gender Gap."[22]

Democrats were not alone in their new attention to the gender factor. Speaking to the inaugural meeting of the Republican Women's Leadership Forum, Edward J. Rollins, political adviser to the Reagan administration, noted, "The gender gap is part of an enormous wave of demographic change sweeping the country that threatens to swamp the Republican party," and "White House polling had found a difference of nine percentage points between women's and men's party preferences, and the sense of urgency . . . was real."[23] The gender gap, and politicians' reactions to it, bolstered arguments made by NOW's leadership that electoral politics constituted the mechanism necessary to further the feminist agenda.

Despite outgoing president Smeal's personal reluctance to revive the ERA, the national NOW board resolved to continue to work on the issue at a February 1983 meeting. Rather than launch a fully renewed ERA campaign, NOW leaders wanted to use candidates' positions on the issue as a signal to voters in the upcoming elections.[24] Newly elected NOW president Judy Goldsmith said, "We are adamant about getting a vote on the E.R.A. in the House and the Senate before the elections . . . women have a right to know where their representatives stand on the E.R.A."[25]

Electoral candidates took note of NOW's political prominence. At the 1983 national NOW conference all six Democratic presidential candidates—Senators Alan Cranston, John Glenn, Gary Hart, and Ernest Hollings, and former senator George McGovern and former vice president Walter Mondale—pledged to consider a woman for vice president.[26] The National Women's Political Caucus experienced similar success in attracting presidential candidates.[27] Gary Hart "began his campaign with a 'women's strategy,' which included, as a part of his basic speech, an acknowledgment of the political power of women."[28] For his part, Mondale "said he would not choose anyone who is not a feminist" for the vice presidential nomination.[29] Mondale also repeatedly spoke with NOW leaders when his campaign feared the group's endorsement might go to Reverend Jesse Jackson, a latecomer to the presidential race.[30]

Endorsing Walter Mondale

NOW president Goldsmith announced that the group would make its first presidential endorsement in the Democratic primary in 1984 and would press the candidate to choose a female vice president. Goldsmith declared, "Defeating President Reagan was NOW's No. 1 priority."[31]

Within a few months, in December 1983 NOW's national board formally endorsed Walter Mondale in an overwhelming though not unanimous vote.[32] Mondale's campaign had told NOW that it needed assistance in states such as Florida in order to succeed; the campaign hoped to tap into NOW's grassroots networks, funds, political skills, and ability to get bodies out to do such time-consuming chores as door-to-door canvassing.[33] Dr. Janet M. Canterbury, a longtime NOW activist and president of the Florida chapter in 1983, reported that "Florida NOW had been given only $11,000 from the national group and its chapters had only political pocket change . . . [but] we are supplying brains and bodies for this campaign. We can put out a 30,000-piece mailing in one night, sort ZIP codes in our sleep and turn out hundreds of people with our phone banks." A Mondale staffer dubbed the campaign's affiliation with NOW "a good marriage."[34] In return for NOW's endorsement, President Goldsmith understood that Mondale would afford the group an inside track in the campaign and would strongly consider nominating a woman as his running mate.[35]

Once the group endorsed Mondale, NOW leaders set to work to secure a female vice presidential nominee. One problem with persuading the Mondale campaign to select a woman was that according to at least one poll conducted by NBC News, the idea appeared to hold no great appeal for voters, male or female, Democrat or Republican.[36] Yet Goldsmith pressed on, at one point warning Mondale that NOW might engineer an embarrassing nomination from the floor of the convention if he failed to choose a woman as his running mate.

At its 1984 convention NOW passed a resolution echoing this threat, causing consternation among other groups, including the National Women's Political Caucus and the American Nurses Association, which had been working with NOW to secure a woman's nomination to the position. The president of the NWPC said, "I'm not saying there won't be a floor fight or a walkout, but there must be a consensus of the coalition." In a swift reaction to NOW's position, potential vice presidential nominees, including Dianne Feinstein, Patricia Schroeder, and Geraldine Ferraro, publicly refused to accept any nomination from the floor.[37] In a subsequent meeting "twenty-three prominent women" in the political world, including Betty Friedan, met with Mondale. State treasurer of Texas Ann Richards reported, "To a person, we said [to him], it's your choice . . . we said, personally and politically, we will support your decision."[38]

On July 12, 1984, Mondale finally did choose a woman, Representative Geraldine A. Ferraro (Queens, N.Y.), as his running mate, unleashing tremendous excitement among feminist supporters.[39] NOW's threat may have backfired, however, weakening Mondale's campaign against Reagan by providing fodder for conservatives and their organizations, such as the National Right to Life Committee, to argue that Mondale caved to feminist demands.[40]

Post-Mondale Electoral Activism

The failure of the Mondale-Ferraro ticket to win the presidential race in 1984 proved a difficult pill for NOW to swallow. On Smeal's re-election to the office of NOW president in 1985, she recommitted the group to work on state and congressional races. The organization remained relatively aloof from presidential campaign politics, however. In 1988 NOW presented a list of forty-seven qualified women to the Democratic Party to consider for nomination to party positions, including vice president.[41] NOW activists increased their pressure on democrats in the wake of the appointment of Judge Clarence Thomas to the U.S. Supreme Court. One NOW board member warned Democratic incumbents (such as Virginia senator and chairman of the Democratic Senatorial Campaign Committee Charles S. Robb) that they would rue the day they failed to scuttle the Thomas nomination: "Women made the difference in electing the Democratic Senate, particularly the Southern Democrats . . . women have been the most loyal of the Democratic voters. We gave them our votes. We gave them our money. And they gave us Clarence Thomas. We're fed up."[42]

Hoping to use the gender gap as a tool against pro-life activists and the Religious Right in local, state, and national politics, NOW concentrated on ousting antiabortion state and congressional legislators. In 1990 NOW combined electoral politics with grassroots activism by launching its "Freedom Caravan for Women's Lives," barnstorming around Pennsylvania working for feminist candidates' political campaigns. In 1991 NOW recruited and supported women in Louisiana for state legislative races in a year-long project, and in 1992 it kicked off its "Elect Women for a Change" campaign, which brought NOW's organizing resources to bear on elections throughout the country, an effort whose lessons continue to be taught to NOW members today.[43] At its 1992 conference NOW's Political Empowerment Caucus "voted overwhelmingly for [resolutions calling for] gender balance, [for] the creation of an international women's congress to exchange information and provide financial support for women candidates around the world [and] the creation of a third party—without giving any emphasis to participation in traditional politics."[44]

While organizations and members associated with the Christian Right flexed their muscles at the 1992 Republican convention (the Christian Coalition, for example, planned "to send out 40 million voter guides . . . [and] to distribute them in 246,000 churches by Election Day"),[45] journalists nevertheless hailed 1992 as "The Year of the Woman" in races for congressional seats: "No matter how the prognostications play out over whether 1992 is a boom year for women getting elected, this much is already beyond dispute: women's political groups and women candidates are reaping a dramatic increase in contributions."[46] A record 117 women candidates ran for Congress in 1992; 54 won. The proportion of women in Congress jumped from 5.6 to 10 percent. The high visibility of "women's" issues in 1992, including abortion rights and sexual harassment (the latter brought to the forefront in the Clarence Thomas–Anita Hill hearings and in publicity regarding the Navy's "Tailhook" scandal), as well as House ethics scandals largely involving male incumbents and the media's focus on women and politics may all have contributed to women's success in the 1992 elections.[47]

Women political elites, using PACs and feminist organizations such as EMILY's List, successfully garnered support for women candidates in the 1992 election cycle. In 1992, for example, the Feminist Majority embarked on a "Feminization of Power Campaign," which focused on finding and supporting women candidates for political office. As for NOW, it geared itself up for the 1992 elections. At its 1992 annual conference members voted to support NOW's "Elect Women for a Change" campaign, which "had projects running full force in Connecticut, Florida, Georgia and Tennessee, helping feminist candidates win Congressional, state and local primaries."[48] Carol Moseley Braun in Illinois and Barbara Boxer and Dianne Feinstein in California all benefited from funds and activists from NOW chapters and PACs.

The Politics of the Electoral Strategy

The electoral strategy seemed an extremely promising one in the immediate post-ERA period. Yet as national NOW and chapters pursued it, a host of dilemmas inevitably surfaced. Although the flexibility to adjust its goals and tactics may allow an organization to maintain its credibility and visibility with the public during unfavorable political periods, such changes can also instigate internal dissention. While some liberal interest groups turned to business consultants to help them manage their long-term strategic plans in the 1980s, for example, they still faced the need to align their plans with established principles and practices. One consultant noted, "These organizations are established . . . they have bylaws, they have budgets, they have track records. It takes a lot of time and energy to create that, and they don't want to lose it."[49]

In NOW's case its leaders dealt with member concerns about shifting from the "ERA strategy" to the "electoral strategy" after the demise of the ERA in three ways: they focused on increasing the organization's cohesiveness; they emphasized the importance of their guiding principles to their strategy; and they underscored the organization's independence from political parties and from coalition partners. Thus by 1992 a reporter covering a NOW conference could still sense that the organization's members felt bound by a common purpose: "Many of the 700 women present who told their stories and plotted their strategies in small groups . . . took pride in the devil-take-the-hindmost sense of separatism that pervades the organization."[50]

Attention to Issues and Grassroots Activists Addressing members' fears that electoral politics might alienate national NOW from the grassroots activists and diminish national investment in a multitude of issues, NOW leaders vowed to increase communication and information transfers among national NOW, its chapters, and state organizations by paying greater attention to outreach and officer visits. President Goldsmith promised that the organization would "increase and regularize mailings . . . increase the use of audio and video tapes . . . increase officer and activist travel to state and regional conferences . . . and increase the number of conference calls for situational and issue briefings for fast-breaking news."[51]

While arguing that "full equality for women will be achieved only through a three-pronged strategy that includes (1) the politicization of American women, (2) a comprehensive and vigorous campaign to eliminate sex discrimination, and (3) passage of the Equal Rights Amendment," the national board frequently referred to its duty to attend to a wide spectrum of feminist concerns. In the same resolution the board acknowledged, "We reaffirm our commitment for a national program emphasizing the full range of priorities of the organization."[52]

After the ERA campaign folded, NOW's board underscored its continuing commitment to consciousness-raising activities and to educating its members about feminist principles. The 1982 national NOW conference approved a resolution supporting the increase of feminist consciousness-raising within the group, and NOW board members revised the 1983 budget to fund a national consciousness-raising campaign:[53]

> Whereas, new members who are joining NOW in ever-increasing numbers, may join us out of support for a single issue, like the ERA, and may not be aware of the pervasiveness of sexism, racism, anti-Semitism, homophobia, etc., and
>
> Whereas, the implementation of NOW's purpose . . . can best be achieved by increasing the activism and unity of our members,
>
> Whereas, CR is the most successful method of bringing us from the isolation of personal experience to personal awareness of the commonality of injustice perpetuated against women, and . . . CR thereby increased the unity and activism at all levels of NOW;
>
> Therefore . . . this National Conference reaffirms NOW's belief in, and its active commitment, to CR as a tried, proven and effective tool for achieving the above-stated objectives.[54]

At NOW's 1982 conference, at which she succeeded Smeal, Goldsmith pledged to "establish a formal program for both leadership and membership training" and to "expand our national fundraising and provide assistance to states and chapters for their fundraising projects by providing technical assistance and/or seed money."[55] An "antiracism" coordinator and Lesbian Rights Project coordinator were hired to deal with these major issues of controversy and concern to feminists.[56]

Electoral Activism as a Vanguard Strategy   Some other feminist activists and groups felt that focusing on elections would be beneficial precisely because it would be less politically controversial, and perhaps more effective, than openly lobbying for pro-choice legislation at either the state or federal levels. Not only did the abortion rights issue stir conservative organizations to action, surveys of voters suggested that a pro-choice position was not necessarily a winning campaign strategy.

Strategists from both parties, as the *New York Times* noted, learned from 1984 that "the women's vote is not homogenous . . . nor are feminist and women's organizations necessarily the best way to reach the majority of women's voters."[57] Koryne Horbal, longtime party and political activist and founder of the Women's Caucus of the Democratic National Committee, said of the 1982 elections, "This next time we are going to focus not so much on the issue of prochoice as the candidate, who will be prochoice. . . . In many cases people aren't comfortable with one issue, but they will vote for someone who believes in that along with a lot of other issues. It's easier to motivate people around a person rather than an issue." Horbal argued that a defeat such as the one feminists experienced with the Equal Rights Amendment could be averted by recognizing, responding to, and mobilizing around the realities of the political system: "We feel that if we continue concentrating at the grassroots level [in local precincts and districts] this will not happen again."[58]

Countering claims from its members and some leaders that the electoral strategy would moderate NOW's demands, leaders cast the strategy as one that was pushed on them by the failure of the Equal Rights Amendment: it was the "betrayal" of legislators that forced feminists to become active in political campaigns. NOW leaders used the evidence of a gender gap to suggest the possibility that the established order could actually be overthrown if enough women voted and enough feminist candidates ran for and won elective office.

In their appeal to activists Smeal and other leaders used dramatic words such as *fascist* to describe antifeminist political leaders.[59] In addition, the organization emphasized the "empowerment" aspects of the electoral strategy. Echoing sentiments laid out in NOW's Statement of Purpose, leaders argued that women's involvement in electoral politics—as voters, candidates, or campaign workers—meant that they were actively engaged in securing their own rights, free from having to "beg" the existing power structure for legislative scraps.

Political Independence   The plunge into electoral politics, including the endorsement of candidates, brought with it the possibility that NOW's political independence would be undermined. At national, regional, and state conferences and through editorials in the *National NOW Times*, the leadership reassured members that NOW would continue to be nonpartisan and would not confine itself to supporting Democrats for office. Yet, leaders also insisted that Republicans needed to be "neutralized":

> The Equal Rights Amendment Campaign taught us a lesson that we will never forget about American politics. . . . We will never forget that the Republican Party not only deserted women's rights, but it led the attack. . . . This is why in the 1982 elections, very few Republicans can or will be supported by the NOW PACs. . . . This is not to say that NOW/PACs are always against the Republicans. . . . [The] situation is not of our making and not of our choice. . . . The newspapers are making much of the fact that NOW PACs are supporting some men over women. . . . But in 1982 we are not dealing with the most perfect of worlds. We are dealing with what is.[60]

For example, NOW received considerable criticism in 1982 for supporting Frank Lautenberg over Millicent Fenwick in the New Jersey Senate race; Fenwick lost. Although Fenwick was a woman generally supportive of women's issues, NOW leaders considered the political environment in which it was making its endorsements. As Goldsmith argued, "You can't endorse people in a vacuum . . . [her election would have placed] some blatant enemies of women's rights in key committee seats."[61] NOW regularly endorsed male Democratic candidates who supported many of NOW's positions over female Republican candidates who supported only some of its positions.[62]

A dramatic departure from its pledge to remain politically independent occurred in 1983, when, as we have seen, the group decided to endorse a presidential candidate for the first time. Goldsmith justified this shift by arguing that ousting President Ronald Reagan from office was absolutely critical if earlier gains in civil and women's rights were to be salvaged. Arguing that only a dire situation called for diverging from NOW's earlier practice of not endorsing presidential candidates, Goldsmith averred, "If Ronald Reagan were not in the White House—if it were, say, Gerald Ford—we would not be endorsing a candidate."[63]

Despite these justifications, the decision jeopardized NOW's credibility. Conservatives seized on NOW's endorsement as proof that the organization did not speak for all women and that it was not a social movement organization but an interest group seeking special favors from and playing a significant role within the Democratic Party. A spokesperson for the Reagan campaign commented, "That organization is really Democratic, no matter what they say. After all, they came out this year and endorsed Walter Mondale."[64]

Mondale's overwhelming loss to incumbent Ronald Reagan led some Democratic political strategists to conclude that the party's identification with "special interests" had harmed the campaign and that the prominence of the National Organization for Women in the race had actually hurt rather than helped. From NOW's perspective, the disastrous outcome to this race, with its first female vice presidential nominee, led the organization to lie low in the 1988 presidential campaign. It also helped delegitimize Goldsmith's presidency; in NOW's next elections Smeal ran against her and won another term. Ultimately, Goldsmith's diversion from the course of political independence subsequently strengthened the organization's commitment to these founding principles. Goldsmith's experimental gamble with the Mondale campaign showed NOW activists the dangers of political collaboration, making them more likely to resist the temptation in the future. Second, such independence was now effectively forced on NOW, since neither the Republican nor the Democratic Party sought to identify closely with the organization after 1984. "Mondale never forgave us," Smeal commented in a July 2003 interview.[65]

A New Political Party   A social movement group's proposal to create an entirely new political party is a both a testament to an organization's commitment to its political ideals and a sign of its profound political isolation. Smeal floated the idea of a new feminist political party as early as 1982, but it was not until 1989, under NOW president Molly Yard's leadership, that the group proposed seriously to research the implications of such a venture.[66]

Bella Abzug and Eleanor Holmes Norton offered lukewarm support for the idea, but most of NOW's usual allies did not leap at the suggestion of a feminist party. At a meeting of the National Women's Political Caucus, for example,

> members ... rejected a call by [NOW] ... for a study of whether a third party should be formed to support women's rights. Though there was no formal vote on the issue, that sentiment was made clear in formal sessions and in conversations outside. "To divert yourself from the established power structure, which will go on and continue to make decisions anyway, to pull yourself out of it, it's absolutely stupid," said Maxine Berman, a Democratic state representative in Michigan. "Everybody here laughed at that thing," said Lana Pollack, a Democratic state senator in Michigan.[67]

Most political commentators and, perhaps more important, most other feminist leaders, including NWPC president Harriet Woods, scoffed at the idea of a third party, taking Yard herself to task for potentially ruining years of their hard work forging relationships with those inside the Republican and Democratic parties. The press roundly derided NOW's "radical" stance and Yard's outlandish tactics.[68] Yard responded to critics that the measure was grassroots-initiated. Indeed, Ellie Smeal contends that Yard's investment in the Democratic Party (she was a McGovern organizer in 1972 and had worked tirelessly within it to gain gender parity for women, for example) combined with her memory of the 1930s and 1940s (during the Democratic Party's purge of leftist women) made her reluctant to abandon the two-party system.[69]

Despite the outpouring of criticism for the idea, NOW's board set up the Commission on Responsive Democracy to study the feasibility of establishing a feminist party. After holding a series of "town-hall" meetings in D.C., Texas, Florida, and Minnesota, complete with speakers, workshops, and expert testimony, the commission voted to endorse the creation of the "21st Century Party" in September 1991.[70] Members at NOW's 1992 annual conference likewise voted in favor of the new political party, which would concentrate on social justice issues.[71] "More than 230 members from 30 states [were] in attendance to adopt a constitution and platform. Its founding principles called for women as 52% of the Party's candidates and officers who must reflect the racial and ethnic diversity of the nation; it also called for an expanded Bill of Rights for the 21st century. Dolores Huerta, co-founder and Vice President Emerita of the United Farm Workers of America, was elected National Chair. Eleanor Smeal, president of the Feminist Majority, was elected National Secretary."[72] The 21st Century Party ultimately received fairly wide-ranging support from the other organizations that participated in the three-year study of the third-party strategy, but its first convention in D.C. in 1992 was also its last, a result perhaps attributable to Democrat Bill Clinton's successful presidential bid that year. In addition, Cesar Chavez's death pulled Dolores Huerta back into duty at the United Farm Worker's union.[73]

Leadership Crisis

After managing the defeat of the ERA, NOW faced a second major challenge. Although the group ended the ratification campaign flush with funds, just three years later it was nearly bankrupt. NOW's financial problems became linked with leadership troubles as well, as NOW president Goldsmith came under fire at the group's confrontational annual conference elections in 1985.

Judy Goldsmith, Ellie Smeal's successor, had served as executive vice president in Smeal's administration. An instructor of English literature, Goldsmith won the presidency in 1982 by a wide margin against candidates such as Sonia Johnson, one of a group of eight women who had fasted for thirty-seven days for the ratification of the Equal Rights Amendment.[74] Like her predecessor, Goldsmith underscored the need for the organization to maintain the political resources it acquired during the ERA campaign: "We must capitalize on the strong foundation that has been laid, and take advantage of the extraordinary momentum and opportunities that now exist. . . . The assaults of the Right Wing on women's rights will only be halted with the defeat of the Reagan forces at the voting booth. To that end, I am committed to the political mobilization that will clearly establish us as a nationwide independent political force."[75]

NOW activists increasingly began to question the actions of Goldsmith and her team, however. When the national board endorsed Walter Mondale for president in December 1983, NOW leaders "hoped it would give them access to Mondale's campaign and a chance to provide some input on issues and tactics."[76] But the endorsement and Goldsmith's connections with the campaign drew fire from members, who called her a "puppet of the Democratic party." Goldsmith's enthusiasm for the national political spotlight appeared to symbolize the national organization's repudiation of its grassroots members and its principle of maintaining political independence. NOW members told the press that "once the en-dorsement was secured, Mr. Mondale ignored NOW and that the endorsement cost the group leverage within the presidential campaign." California NOW members, for example, were disappointed with the number of NOW members chosen to be Mondale delegates. " 'Was it a mistake?' asks Toni Carabillo, an editor of NOW's bimonthly national newspaper. 'It may have been.' "[77] By courting Mondale and working to influence his nomination of Geraldine Ferraro for vice president, Goldsmith "did not win . . . kudos from her comrades." Even a Washington lobbyist in regular contact with women's organizations could clearly see the problem: "NOW is about being on the outside and shaking the foundations of the ruling class . . . Judy misunderstood the role of the organization. She went to dinner at the Mondales' and got drummed out of the corps."[78]

Mondale's selection of Geraldine Ferraro as his running mate, though an exciting and symbolic win for feminists, lost its luster as the campaign subsequently ignored women's issues and advised Ferraro to play them down as well. Ultimately, Mondale's campaign contributed little to the feminist cause.[79] It also appeared that the 1984 "year of the woman" in electoral politics was not nearly as successful as women's rights supporters had hoped.[80] Democrats blamed Mondale's association with feminists and other interest groups for his failure.[81]

Financial problems also loomed: as Goldsmith's first term as NOW president drew to a close, insiders began to realize that NOW was in serious need of a cash infusion.[82] Although repeatedly warned by those with access to the financial data, Goldsmith apparently was unwilling to cut spending to comport with new funding realities facing the organization after the ERA campaign ended. The national board repeatedly asked for financial statements, which she did not provide.

In January 1985, about six months before NOW's 1985 presidential elections, NOW members who felt discontented with the organization's direction and who knew of its precarious financial situation (which, despite dues from eight hundred chapters, included overdue payments to vendors were mounting)[83] asked former president Smeal to help save the organization from bankruptcy and to run for president. Complicating the matter was the fact that Smeal and her supporters did not want to publicize NOW's financial problems for fear of press attention and further loss of support from members and donors. In addition, some activists, including Friedan, protested that Smeal was trying to take over the organization.[84] Others, like the president of New York City NOW, worried that

Smeal's re-election would reduce national's investment in local initiatives: "Judy has done an excellent job in helping local chapters organize for women's rights in their own communities . . . if Ellie is elected, I'm afraid NOW would again focus on national actions in Washington."[85]

Smeal argued that she and Goldsmith agreed on issues but not on tactics. One reporter said the schism between Goldsmith and Smeal "could be characterized . . . as coalition versus confrontation." The members who urged Smeal to run hoped the organization would become "more outspoken, assertive and publicly active." Smeal proposed a campaign to pass a state ERA in Vermont, which could serve as a template for other state legislatures. In response, Goldsmith (echoing Smeal's own words in 1982) countered that until feminist legislators filled those seats, a revival of ERA campaigns would prove fruitless. (In fact, the measure ultimately failed in Vermont.) In defense of her leadership style, Goldsmith declared, "Loud may be good, but it is not the only level of decibels that is heard."[86]

In the end, Smeal's record of service to NOW, in addition to her stated plans to combine massive demonstrations and protests with full-blown electoral activism, won her election by 136 of the 839 votes cast. (Smeal reportedly spent $18,000 on campaign expenses; Goldsmith, $14,000.) Smeal credited a surge of grassroots support and campaigning for her candidacy: "When I started [my campaign] I had commitments from some very large states, including Pennsylvania, Florida and California, and all those people worked very, very hard." A member of Goldsmith's team, executive vice president Lois Galgay Reckitt, may also have boosted Smeal's campaign by endorsing her immediately before the election.[87]

Referring to Goldsmith's preferred tactics of legislative lobbying and coalition building, Smeal said, "We tried that last year—but now it's time to go back into the streets."[88] Ramping up her rhetoric, Smeal declared, "The worst thing we can do right now is try to become acceptable."[89] As NOW was at least $1 million in debt when Smeal regained office,[90] she worked to cut the organization's expenses and successfully negotiated a bridge loan to pay its vendors. She also reestablished an arms-length relationship with the Democratic Party, since Goldsmith's attempts to go "along with the establishment of the Democratic Party" in order to defeat President Reagan "didn't work."[91] "Mrs. Smeal said she viewed it as 'imperative' that the women's movement stay politically independent, arguing, 'we're going to have to depend on ourselves.'"[92]

The Growing Clout of the Right and Threats to *Roe v. Wade*

The third prominent crisis NOW faced in these years involved the rising influence of conservatism in American politics. The New Right consolidated its gains from the 1970s and early 1980s, helping win, for example, the reelection of President Ronald Reagan and the subsequent election of his vice president, George Herbert Walker Bush, to the presidency in 1988. Among the most dramatic effects of conservative political influence from NOW's point of view was the significant threat to women's reproductive rights.

Supreme Court Appointments

A string of retirements from the Supreme Court offered the Republican administrations of Ronald Reagan and George W. Bush significant opportunities to attempt to move the Court to the right. President Reagan appointed William Rehnquist to the position of chief justice in 1986; Rehnquist presided over a group that included four new Republican appointees (Anthony Kennedy, David Souter, Antonin Scalia, and Clarence Thomas) over the course of the next five years. NOW protested each of these choices in addition to the failed 1987 nomination of Robert Bork, calling them "disastrous" for women's rights and warning that *Roe v. Wade* was imperiled.

None of the Reagan and Bush nominees to the Supreme Court could demonstrate reassuring records on *Roe v. Wade*, civil rights, or women's rights to the proponents of those causes. Nevertheless, after the much-publicized success of a liberal coalition that helped derail the nomination of Robert Bork to the Court in 1987, NOW sometimes found itself fighting against subsequent nominations without a great deal of support from other progressive groups. Molly Yard declared NOW's decision to oppose Anthony Kennedy's nomination, in contrast to other groups that decided to tread more cautiously, not wanting to risk the credibility won in the Bork fight. NARAL president Kate Michelman said, "Obviously, I want and our members want NARAL to continue to be in the forefront, to have its voice heard . . . but I need to balance that. Our work enhanced our image as a mainstream, effective organization [after the Bork nomination fight] and I don't want to dissipate any of that." Yard countered, "I'm not sure how it plays . . . but we would have been negligent in our duty if we hadn't said it."[93]

Three years later NOW was also one of the few organizations to quickly organize opposition to the appointment of former attorney general and Supreme Court justice for New Hampshire David H. Souter to the Court.[94] Similarly, in 1991 NOW's acting president, Patricia Ireland (Yard was recuperating from a stroke), "became the first leader of a civil rights organization" to oppose President Bush's nomination of Judge Clarence Thomas.[95] Other civil rights groups found it difficult to rally against Thomas despite his views against affirmative action because they wanted to support an African American on the Court. The NAACP delayed taking a position. Although it ultimately decided to oppose him, a leader of the group's regional office in Atlanta said, "Instead of a flag-waving, foot-stomping appeal, we are going to have to take a more demure approach."[96] Allegations regarding Thomas's behavior toward law professor Anita Hill when both were employed at the Equal Employment Opportunity Commission led to explosive Senate Judiciary hearings, but they did not derail Thomas's confirmation.

Judicial Rulings

Generally speaking, Supreme Court decisions between 1989 and 2000 upheld the basic tenets of *Roe v. Wade*. The Court upheld fixed "buffer zones" around abortion clinics that ensured clients could enter without hindrance by antiabortion protesters. However, four of nine justices consistently argued that the right to abortion was not constitutionally guaranteed, resulting at times in only bare majorities upholding the right to choose abortion as outlined by *Roe v. Wade.* The Court also upheld an increasing number of state statutes restricting the provision of abortion services.

During this period the Court upheld earlier rulings that permitted the states and the federal government to prohibit the use of state or federal funds to pay for abortions not medically necessary to preserve the health of the mother. In addition, the Supreme Court overturned portions of previous decisions supporting abortion rights, including *City of Akron v. Akron Center for Reproductive Health* (1983) and *Thornburgh v. American College of Obstetricians and Gynecologists* (1986).[97]

Yet the Supreme Court's 1989 decision in *Webster v. Reproductive Health Services* confirmed the fears of pro-choice organizations. In this ruling the Court held constitutional state statutes that prevented abortions from being performed in public hospitals and denied public funding of abortions. In other words, states now had freer rein to place restrictions on abortion providers and patients seeking them. The *Webster* decision sent shock waves throughout the feminist community and caused states' rights and antiabortion advocates to claim victory. Feminist organizations experienced a surge in members and contributions; NOW gained forty thousand members between April and July 1989, according to Yard.[98] By July 1990 NOW claimed 270,000 members and its financial position stabilized. As a result of the *Webster* decision and the Clarence Thomas/Anita Hill confrontation, the groups collected donations exceeding $10 million.[99]

Yard announced a massive reproductive rights demonstration to take place in November 1989, but leaders of other groups such as NARAL hesitated to expend resources on another march. (Yard did not consult with other organizations before her announcement.)[100] NARAL's liaison coordinator said, "It's such an enormous amount of work to pull off something like this . . . it's all-consuming. A lot of groups thought, 'Is this the best thing we could be doing right now?'"[101] However, NOW and other pro-choice organizations agreed to fund a counterattack to the *Webster* decision, pooling their mailing lists to reach the largest possible number of donors.[102]

In 1991's *Rust v. Sullivan* the Court upheld the so-called gag rule supported by the Reagan and Bush administrations. This gag rule made it illegal for medical personnel to advise women about the legality and availability of abortion services. NOW chapter activists across the country "shadowed President Bush, Vice President Quayle, and Secretary Sullivan wherever they spoke. At the public speaking events, NOW activists protested by wearing white gags on their mouths and holding signs that read 'Overturn the Gag Rule.'"[103] The Court's 1992 decision in *Planned Parenthood of Southeastern Pennsylvania v. Casey,* though nominally upholding *Roe,* legitimated the government's interest in the fetus throughout a pregnancy. *Casey* overturned significant portions of Supreme Court decisions in *Akron* and *Thornburgh.*

> By a vote of 7–2, the Court upheld provisions of a Pennsylvania statute that required (1) physicians to provide patients with anti-abortion information, including pictures of fetuses at various stages of development to discourage women from obtaining abortions; (2) a mandatory 24-hour delay following these lectures; (3) the filing of reports, available for public inspection and copying, including the name and location of any facility performing abortions that receives any state funds; and (4) a one-parent consent requirement for minors with a judicial bypass.[104]

NOW began a civil disobedience campaign in 1992 in response to the *Casey* decision, making an effort to match the direct-action tactics of antiabortion activists with its own rallies and marches.[105]

Republican Administrations, Conservative Legislatures

For NOW, the Reagan administration's stance on women's rights was demonstrated by its 1984 order barring U.S. nonprofit groups such as Planned Parenthood from offering abortion-related information or aid to overseas health organizations. Reagan regularly expressed his public support for this cause at pro-life rallies.[106] As attacks and bomb threats on abortion clinics increased, NOW and other women's groups became frustrated with what they viewed as Reagan's weak denunciations of such activities.

The first Bush administration also proved a stalwart supporter of those seeking to undermine *Roe v. Wade.* For example, in an unusual move, the Justice Department supported Operation Rescue in its attempt to overturn an injunction preventing it from blocking access to abortion clinics. In addition, despite the Democrat-controlled Congress's attempt to repudiate the "gag rule," Congress was unable to muster the two-thirds vote necessary to overcome Bush's vetoes.[107]

In 1988 federal regulations required "recipients of Federal family planning money . . . to tell their clients nothing about abortion except that it is wrong."[108] Abortion rights appeared to be eroding around the country. A survey conducted by NARAL found that 24 state legislatures "favored making abortion illegal"; 17 states were divided, and only 9 states were clearly pro-choice.[109] In the early 1990s state legislatures around the country considered and passed legislative restrictions on abortion rights, including such measures as required parental notification, the institution of waiting periods, and the outright banning of abortion except in cases of serious danger to the mother.[110]

The Pro-Life Movement

Pro-life organizations gained in strength and visibility during this period, some using dramatic grassroots tactics such as blocking health clinic entrances to stop women from entering to receive services. Other organizations, such as the National Right to Life Committee, vowed to prevent the importation of the early abortion pill, RU-486, from France.[111] Antiabortion activists Randall Terry, Joseph Scheidler, and their organizations the Pro-Life Action League (founded in 1980), the Pro-Life Action Network (founded in 1985), and Operation Rescue (founded in 1986) forged close ties. Operation Rescue (OR), headed by Terry, boasted 125 affiliates and employed violent tactics including the bombing of women's health clinics. In 1992 OR staged protests at the Democratic and Republican conventions.

Beginning in the mid-1980s members of these organizations actively supported, mobilized, and participated in clinic protests and blockades. Some waged violent attacks on abortion providers: "By Federal count, there have been 30 instances of bombing, firebombing and arson at abortion clinics since May 1982."[112] Three years later the National Abortion Federation reported "224 acts of violence . . . against abortion clinics throughout the country," constituting what Smeal called "a reign of terror."[113]

NOW responded to these activities with large demonstrations, legal prosecution, and grassroots mobilization to help keep clinics open. Before she left office, in response to a federal warning about potential attacks on abortion clinics, NOW president Goldsmith announced in 1985 that the group would undertake a vigil at approximately two dozen clinics to confront what they called the antiabortion "bullies." (The National Abortion Federation protested, arguing that NOW members were imperiling people in order to get publicity.)[114] One of Smeal's first organizational initiatives when she took over from Goldsmith was to hold a march on Washington for reproductive rights in April 1986 which attracted approximately 100,000 people.[115] NOW and other abortion-rights groups held large demonstrations in Washington again in April 1989, November 1989, and April 1992.

In addition to beginning work to secure the legalization of RU 486, a medication intended to be used in the first eight weeks of pregnancy to induce abortion chemically, NOW sought other solutions to the problem of the blockades and violent attacks against abortion clinics and providers. In 1986 NOW's newly created foundation brought a class-action lawsuit on behalf of NOW, abortion clinics, and "all women who might seek to use their services." Employing the Racketeer-Influenced and Corrupt Organizations Act (RICO), *NOW v. Scheidler* alleged that "Joseph Scheidler, Randall Terry, Operation Rescue, and other anti-abortion groups and zealots are the organizers of a nationwide network coordinating violent attacks against abortion providers."[116] In 1992 a federal court dismissed the case, reasoning that because the defendants did not have an economic motive in their activities, they could not be sued under federal racketeering laws. (The Supreme Court overturned the lower court's decision in 1994.)

In 1989 President Yard also announced that NOW would mount a major effort to defend abortion clinics.[117] NOW, the YWCA,

Planned Parenthood (which raised money for clinic defense), Mary Dent Crisp's National Republican Coalition for Choice, and local pro-choice groups worked with Smeal's Feminist Majority Foundation (which had developed its own "Clinic Defense Project" capable of sending organizers around the country to clinics experiencing attacks) to formulate a systematic strategy to defend clinics. The groups sought to prevent Operation Rescue activists from chaining themselves in front of clinic doors and taught volunteers how to resist pro-life activists' attacks nonviolently.[118] Before OR's planned action against women's clinics during the 1992 Democratic convention, NOW and the Feminist Majority worked in coalition: "Advance teams from the Feminist Majority, led by Katherine Spillar, went to New York weeks before the convention at the invitation of local groups who wanted to learn the successful tactics that had been used in Buffalo. Feminist Majority organizers worked with the New York Clinic Defense Task Force training and mobilizing thousands of clinic defenders. Constantly covering up to 35 of the city's 151 clinics at a time, up to 3,000 clinic defenders kept all clinic doors open during OR's attempted blockades."[119]

NOW and other groups mounted several successful legal challenges to organizations such as Operation Rescue. Despite the Bush administration's support (through the Justice Department) of OR's blocking of access to clinic entrances, as in Wichita, Kansas, in 1991, NOW had begun to erode the work of OR and its leaders through court injunctions and fines. In 1990 OR leader Randall Terry announced that the financial effects of these court decisions were forcing him to close his national headquarters in New York.[120] And at NOW's 1992 annual conference members endorsed "a strategy to step up non-violent civil disobedience actions" to protect abortion rights.[121]

NOW and Progressive Groups: Struggles over Strategy

Of the three major challenges NOW faced between 1982 and 1992, perhaps the one that tested the integrity of its principles and practices most seriously was the growth in the political power of conservatives.[122] In this context we might expect to see NOW hew more closely to its allies in other feminist and progressive organizations and to the Democratic Party. When NOW leaders could justify such coalitions, they participated enthusiastically in them. But just as frequently, NOW found itself outside the "mainstream" of liberal groups because it was more vocal, more demanding, and less willing to compromise.

Internal Conflicts over the Focus on Abortion Rights

After the 1989 *Webster* decision, most feminist organizations, including NOW, focused heavily on abortion rights. Although Bella Abzug, former representative from New York and cofounder of the National Women's Political Caucus, said "abortion is the Vietnam of this generation," some NOW members and political commentators complained that the group was paying too much attention to the issue.[123] NOW had invested a great deal between 1982 and 1992 on preserving *Roe v. Wade*; however, an account of the 1992 national NOW conference (its theme: "Strength in Diversity") suggests that overall, members and leaders were still concerning themselves with a fairly broad range of issues:

> Resolutions passed by the conference included: endorsement of NOW's "Elect Women For A Change" campaign; a strategy to step up non-violent civil disobedience actions in support of legal abortion; opposition to anti-lesbian and gay ballot measures such as those in Colorado and Oregon; and a campaign to pressure the Department of Defense to make a full investigation into the Tailhook incident. Conference delegates also voted to endorse the 21st Century Party, the creation of which was proposed by NOW's Commission for Responsive Democracy in 1991. NOW President Patricia Ireland, Executive Vice President Kim Gandy, Secretary Ginny Montes and Action Vice President Rosemary Dempsey also led a NOW delegation of more than 250 activists in Chicago's Gay Pride March.[124]

Other NOW members and leaders questioned the wisdom of the clinic defense projects that many chapters had developed. A "Chapter Development Report" (issued by then Executive Vice President Kim Gandy) from the early 1990s reminds activists, "the temptation to engage in service-oriented activities is great, for much of this work needs to be done. . . . Organizationally, social services represent a 'band aid' approach to the problems faced by women in this society. Although NOW possesses the most comprehensive feminist agenda of any organization, it does not focus on service activities [or offer] aid to individual women in achieving . . . temporary relief from oppression."

NOW activists frustrated with the abortion rights focus were not alone. Some African American women and women of color felt that the emphasis on this issue failed to reflect their own primary concerns, such as infant mortality and forced sterilization (despite the fact that the abortion rate was higher for nonwhite women than white women).[125] Leaders of the ACLU and of women's rights organizations, including the National Black Women's Health Project, the National Women's Political Caucus, and even Planned Parenthood, all found they had to defend their abortion-rights activism to their members.[126] In the case of the ACLU the abortion-rights section ultimately split from the main group to form the Center for Reproductive Law and Policy in 1992.[127]

External Criticism of NOW's Abortion Rights Focus

Although other pro-choice groups faced a measure of internal dissent as a result of their focus on reproductive rights, the National Organization for Women seemed to draw the largest number of external critics on this score. Betty Friedan had long argued for a more family- and child-oriented strategy for the women's movement, and after 1987 her points were echoed by others.[128] Political commentator Sally Quinn noted, "Like Communism in the former Soviet Empire . . . the movement in its present form has outlasted its usefulness."[129]

In contrast to what seemed like NOW's incessant doomsday chorus about the end of *Roe v. Wade*, a few political insiders, including Eleanor Holmes Norton and Ann Richards, began to argue that women's most immediate, basic concerns involved not abortion rights but economic, family, and child-care issues, and that feminist groups should focus on these.[130] As Patricia Ireland rose to the office of NOW president, political observers suggested that because of the group's "radicalism," its "unremitting indignation," and its reluctance to participate in legislative compromise, the organization was an anachronism.

When confronted about accusations that the National Organization for Women was too radical, the group's new president demonstrated her awareness of NOW's place in the universe of progressive organizations. Ireland declared "sharply": "We lead public opinion, we do not follow it . . . that's who we are. Sure, it has its down side. Taking a leadership position makes people uncomfortable."[131]

NOW was urged in vain by liberal organizations to tone down its tactics and rhetoric in the 1980s and early 1990s because of the Republican stranglehold on politics. When pro-choice Democratic candidate Bill Clinton won the 1992 presidential race, feminist groups and sympathetic politicians again advised NOW to moderate its goals and tactics to avoid offending the new administration. Though Ireland worked to build stronger bridges between NOW and like-minded groups, NOW remained stubbornly outside the mainstream.

7. The Clinton Years and Beyond

For over thirty-five years, NOW has followed
a simple yet profoundly important guiding principle:
that organizing at the grass roots—mobilizing individuals
to take action—is the single most effective way to create
fundamental and lasting social change for women.

Kim Gandy

The National Organization for Women continues to be a lightning
rod for critics of the feminist movement. It earns the wrath of those
who feel the group is too radical, too uncompromising in its focus on
abortion rights "on demand" and on the rights of lesbian and gays,
to the exclusion of the concerns of "average" women, such as pay
equity, family and child-care issues, and employment discrimination.
At the same time, the organization is denounced in other quarters for
not investing enough in issues other than those concerning white,
middle-class, middle-aged, professional women.

There is a grain of truth in some of these claims. Led by Patricia
Ireland (1991–2001) and Kim Gandy (2001–), NOW has not moder-
ated its policy goals, to the chagrin of many allies. The group frequently pressured President Clinton on his positions, particularly on
his plans to reform the welfare system. Despite drops in membership
and funds (declines that many other organizations experienced as
well) after Clinton's election, NOW did not attempt to gain new

members by modifying its stances on issues such as gay rights or the legality of "late-term" or "partial-birth" abortions.

Ireland and Gandy continued to extend and reinforce NOW's electoral strategy, holding voter registration and mobilization drives. In place of moderating NOW's goals or seeking mainstream approval from the public or from politicians, however, Ireland and Gandy pursued a different set of tactics. Under their leadership the organization worked to attract new adherents such as younger feminists on college campuses. Although it is often isolated from coalition work with liberal feminist groups because of its unwillingness to yield to legislative compromises, NOW is strengthening its ties to the lesbian and gay community, to organizations advocating for ethnic and racial minorities, to labor unions, and to groups working on behalf of the poor.

NOW has not so far invested a great deal in ways to ease the work-family "juggling act" that some have argued is the basis of a revived feminist movement. The organization's concerns in the area of children and families are the physical and economic threats faced by women in poverty, countering what it sees as a regressive "father's rights" movement, and the enforcement of child support orders.

President Clinton

Even before his election, Bill Clinton's record and agenda never thrilled NOW. Although his pro-choice position was encouraging, his "New Democrat" economic policies drew fire from NOW activists. Nevertheless, Clinton's election resulted in some changes sought by feminist and liberal groups, including passage of the long-awaited Family and Medical Leave Act in 1993, passage of the Violence Against Women Act in 1994, and the appointment of women to prominent posts, such as Ruth Bader Ginsburg to the Supreme Court, Janet Reno as attorney general, and Hazel O'Leary as secretary of energy.

Despite these victories, leaders of groups such as the Women's Legal Defense Fund and the National Women's Political Caucus interpreted the political environment as one calling for moderation in liberals' discourse and tactical choices, given Clinton's conservatism and lack of support in Congress.[1] Reflecting the more conservative mood of the country, the National Abortion Rights Action League (NARAL) added the phrase "reproductive rights" to its name in 1993. A decade later the word "abortion" disappeared from the organization's name, which is now NARAL Pro Choice America. President Michelman argued, "I'm okay if someone calls this moderate. I just know it's right."[2]

NOW leaders disagreed with this strategy. On hearing from insiders that Clinton might not follow through on his promises to appoint substantial numbers of women to public office, for example, they quickly sent the message to the president that they were not going to maintain a decorous silence, leading Clinton to castigate them as feminist "bean counters."[3]

NOW's concerns about Clinton's support for women's economic security came to the forefront as it became clear that he would support major reforms in welfare, including the largest program, Aid to Families with Dependent Children (AFDC). NOW staged a (poorly reported) twenty-one-day vigil and fast in front of the White House before the passage of what it called the "punitive" Personal Responsibility and Work Opportunity Act of 1996. When Clinton signed the bill, which not only allowed states to place a time limit on welfare assistance but also restricted assistance to legal immigrants and whittled away at the food stamp program, Republican senator Bob Dole noted: "He's done everything but change parties."[4]

As a result of Clinton's support for this bill, NOW/PAC would not support his 1996 reelection bid. In an article in the *National NOW Times* titled "Clinton: Our Option, Not Our Answer," Ireland outlined Clinton's failures. In addition to welfare reform, they included attempts to undermine funding for the Violence Against Women Act and his "so-called compromise" regarding the "Don't Ask, Don't Tell" policy on gays in the military. She wrote, "Clinton may be the option for some of us again this election year, but he's not the answer. We are. At a time when some argue for a return to narrow, single-issue politics or feel they cannot stomach electoral politics at all, NOW's direction continues to be toward deepening the ties among progressive movements and moving more of us into elected office."[5]

Despite this pledge, NOW soon ran into trouble as a result of its measured response to allegations that Clinton sexually harassed Paula Jones when he was governor of Arkansas, in addition to Juanita Brodderick's and Kathleen Willey's allegations of sexual assault by the president. Although NOW issued at least nineteen statements and press releases between May 1994 and February 1999 denouncing what it saw as the right wing's exploitation of these women for political purposes and encouraging the full investigation of the allegations, the organization had difficulty convincing pundits that it had not abandoned its integrity in a pragmatic effort to support a pro-choice Democratic president.[6] Ironically, feminists' success in attracting attention to the problem of sexual harassment, so vividly evidenced by the resignation of Republican Senator Robert Packwood in 1995, made them easy targets for conservatives, who asked why NOW did not rush to demand Clinton's resignation.

Conservatives argued that NOW had abandoned its feminist principles and had thereby lost its "moral authority" and political independence, since it had proved itself a pawn of the Democratic Party.[7] In April 1998 Ireland responded by noting, "NOW is an independent political force that believes feminist principles trump practical politics. Our political action committee did not endorse in the presidential races of 1992 and 1996, and we have organized many protests over policy differences with the Clinton administration."[8] In a 2003 interview, Ireland maintained that, "women overwhelmingly did not want impeachment, so it was important for us to echo that. It cost us; everyone jumped all over that. . . . I would do it again."[9]

Perhaps the most strident reaction to NOW's official position came from within the organization, however. The Dulles (Virginia)–area NOW chapter tried to unite formally with the Independent Women's Forum (a conservative woman's organization) to protest NOW's position and statements regarding the Paula Jones case. This chapter, headed by Marie-Jose Ragab (a former national

NOW staff member and contributor to the *National NOW Times*), released a statement to the press in June 1998: "We continue to be chagrined at the lack of leadership from National NOW on sexual harassment, which has jeopardized the overall credibility of the women's movement. . . . Therefore, we maintain our call for [NOW officers'] immediate resignation."[10] In spite of this denunciation, criticism from other chapters, states, or regions regarding the Clinton matter or the Dulles chapter's allegations was generally mild where it existed at all.

Responses to Membership Challenges

In 1992 NOW reported 275,000 members.[11] The memberships of many voluntary associations including the League of Women Voters, the NAACP, the Christian Coalition, and the NWPC, declined in the 1990s. In NOW's case, membership declined by approximately 10 percent a year between 1992 and 2000.[12] Officially, NOW claims between 550 and 600 chapters; in 2003 I estimated the number at 405.[13] Many of these chapters have fewer than one hundred members; frequently, their "offices" are located in a chapter president's home. Like many activist organizations, chapters generally have a core of fewer than twenty-five active members.[14]

NOW still relies almost exclusively on membership outreach for its income. The national office retains less than half the normal membership dues of $35 (individuals can also pay dues based on a sliding scale adjusted for income level). Because of the cost of direct mail, most of NOW's revenue comes from membership renewals rather than new members. In 1997 NOW's foundation subsidized approximately 25 percent of the salaries of the four national NOW officers; the foundation's total budget was only about $500,000.[15]

These facts help explain why dips in the membership rolls are serious business for NOW and why the group's officers and board members have strong incentives to keep the interests of members in mind. In response to the membership declines of the 1990s, NOW organized six "summits" over ten years: Young Feminist Summits in

1991, 1995, and 1997; a Women of Color and Allies Summit in 1998; an ERA Summit in 1995, and a Lesbian Rights Summit in 1999. These summits were partially underwritten by the NOW Foundation and included the types of activities that characterized the 1991 Young Feminist Summit: "Young feminists from all over the country converged on Akron, OH, for NOW's Young Feminist Conference that attracted 750 participants from 42 states. Conference participants attended workshops and issue hearings, discussed, debated, caucused and passed resolutions, signed up for campus action teams, internships and field organizing work and organized a zap action to demonstrate their opposition to the Persian Gulf War."[16]

The advantage of such summits is that they bring together many like-minded organizations and women and men unaffiliated with any group while they energize communities and raise consciousness. However, at least in the short term, NOW has had trouble translating this energy into membership growth. In addition, unlike NOW's annual conferences, these summits do not produce policy that leads to concrete action.

To directly boost its membership, NOW undertook a "Mega-Membership Drive" in 1997 and again in 1998, offering prizes to chapters for every ten new members recruited by a state organization or local chapter.[17] In 1986 NOW's annual budget was $6,300,000;[18] in 1997, by comparison, NOW's expenses amounted to a bit less than $6 million.[19] Karen Johnson, vice president for membership, noted the benefits of the drive: "We know that the new members who are most likely to become local activists are those who are recruited by and affiliated with a local NOW chapter, and that's why we're committed to making this membership drive a big success."[20] By the end of the 1997 drive, even with the added incentive of additional prizes, only 42 of about 405 chapters (or about 10.4 percent) "qualified for the prize drawing by recruiting at least ten members each and 16 of those chapters qualified for multiple chances."[21]

NOW also focused on improving communications between national NOW leaders and staff and local chapters and state organizations. The *National NOW Times* publicized a new "Activist Liaison System" in its fall 1998 and winter 1999 issues. This service was "designed to improve communication between the activists in the field and the activists in the Action center with periodic updates on important issues and campaigns." Setting aside a time for the National Action Center to be available to chapters and activists also allows the national office to "troubleshoot any communication problems a chapter or state is having with the Action Center."[22]

Finally, NOW began to improve its technological outreach, in part with funds from tax-deductible donations to the NOW Foundation. In the mid-1990s NOW created a Web presence and as of 2004 has more than three thousand documents available. It is also able to communicate with its chapter and state leaders through Web pages accessible only to chapter, state, and regional presidents and officers.[23]

One sign of NOW's maturation as an organization is its establishment of a tax-deductible 501(c)(3) foundation, created in 1986. NOW and the NOW Foundation "are sister organizations, sharing some staff and office space. Patricia Ireland is the president of both organizations and they have overlapping officers and board." The foundation's purpose is to "advance women's rights and promote the goal of equality in the United States and around the world through education, litigation, advocacy, networking, conferences, publications, training and leadership development."[24]

The foundation sponsored most if not all of the educational and networking summits NOW held in the 1990s. Leadership training is an important aspect of the foundation's work; it conducts workshops for NOW's own activists as well as community and campus activists on organizing techniques and on substantive issues such as women's health and prejudice reduction. The foundation's educational focus also allows NOW to underwrite NOW officers' travel around the country to give speeches and presentations. The foundation was active as well in the *NOW v. Scheidler* case, using the Racketeer-Influenced and Corrupt Organizations Act (RICO) against antiabortion activists. "Stop the Rescue Racket" collected detailed information on antiabortion activists and their networks and activities.[25]

Some NOW activists question national NOW's relationship with its foundation and the fact that a portion of the NOW's staff's salaries are paid through the foundation. Others point to a campaign the foundation initiated entitled "Love Your Body Day," funded by an outside grant and widely promoted by national NOW staff, as an example of how the leadership's time and energy can be siphoned away by foundation projects. As these members emphasize, no grass-roots activists called for such a campaign; it was undertaken only because the grant specifies such a campaign. Dissenters reason that in order to maintain the highest accountability of leadership and staff, NOW and not the NOW Foundation should provide for all the national NOW's salaries.[26] Others object that the project appears to encourage women to see themselves—rather than social norms, constraints, and an inegalitarian power structure—as the roadblocks to equality. A flyer expressing this opinion "was distributed at the 1995 Young Feminist Summit to protest the idea that women's equality can be achieved through health, self-esteem, and positive body image."[27]

Goals and Tactics

Although NOW is often criticized for its goals and tactics by other women's groups who urge moderation, other activists charge NOW with being too wedded to the middle-of-the-road. By mid-1992 several new women's organizations formed to take radical action to undermine the political power structure and to address the policy needs of women of African American descent, women of ethnic minorities, young women, and women living in poverty, including the Women's Health Action and Mobilization (WHAM) and the Women's Action Coalition (WAC). These groups contended that their small, less hierarchical structure offered greater flexibility and speed in responding to crises. Rebecca Walker (Alice Walker's daughter) cofounded the Third Wave, a young women's organization that received funding from the Ms. Foundation. Third Wave founders complained that the older white leadership of NOW and other feminist organizations failed to address the concerns of women of color.[28] Leaders of these new groups argued that organizations such as NOW "carry the weight of these stalwart, suited women who are always so serious. But they luncheon more than they demand."[29]

At NOW's 2003 national conference, guest speaker Rebecca Walker castigated members for their adherence to old-fashioned conceptions of feminism, for their failure to listen to young women, and for their foot-dragging on embracing issues of diversity and on speaking out against racism. Walker urged the activists to look beyond the word *feminist*: "More important than calling oneself a feminist is committing feminist acts."[30] Walker's comments revealed a lack of knowledge about NOW's political history.

Before 2003 NOW had also organized young feminist conferences, and the NOW Foundation had specifically addressed concerns of young feminists. The 2003 conference featured a special panel that brought together NOW activists concerned with "intergenerational issues." One speaker said, "What attracted me to NOW—[the group] gave me a voice as a disabled [woman living in] poverty and a lesbian. . . . It changed my life; I have leadership positions. It's very rare to have a multi-issue, broad based group. . . . No other organization gets the connections better than we do. . . . [My work on the] national board is a highlight—that my voice could effect change is a life changing event." At a later plenary session a group of young NOW activists presented a resolution that would dedicate one seat on the national board to a "young feminist," although young feminists (those under thirty) have been members of the board in the past with some regularity. When the group saw that its proposal had little chance of passage, it sought out the guidance of more experienced NOW activists, including Ellie Smeal. Though Smeal did not favor the proposal, she helped the young women secure a "permanent task force" of young feminists "to advise the board of directors and national conference on matters of agenda, leadership recruitment and issue prioritization regarding young feminists in NOW."[31]

In 1992, NOW's foundation helped cofound "Up and Out of Poverty NOW," described in the foundation's annual report as "a coalition of feminists and welfare rights activists working together to ensure that the voices of low-income women are heard. Foundation

staff work closely with welfare rights groups, homeless organizations, anti-hunger groups and immigration groups to fight efforts to
take away basic health care, education, housing and programs to aid
children."[32] The foundation has a Public Policy and Welfare Rights
Project to follow developments in these areas. In 1993 NOW worked
with the National Welfare Rights Union and other organizations to
counter President Clinton's positions on welfare reform.

NOW's activism on behalf of the passage of the 1994 Violence
Against Women Act (VAWA) and later on behalf of its reauthoriza-
tion and full funding in 2000 was also directed at women who are
often in poverty or who may become impoverished and/or homeless
as a result of domestic violence. In 1995 NOW passed a resolution to
fight attempts by California governor Pete Wilson and Newt Gingrich to dismantle affirmative action, and the group continues to
work on this issue.[33] In 1996 national NOW actively resisted what it
called Clinton's "welfare repeal" bill. In 2001 the NOW conference
passed a resolution calling for the organization to "make economic
justice a core priority issue."[34]

NOW also redoubled its efforts to deal with its internal racism. In
December 1995 NOW censured a California chapter leader, Tammy
Bruce, for her racially insensitive comments during the O. J. Simpson
case and publicly apologized for her. Ten board members subsequently issued a statement noting that, "We, the women of color
board members, are constantly confronting apprehension about
NOW within our own communities and are repeatedly compelled to
defend our participation in NOW. . . . The National Organization
for Women is an organization that is deeply committed to racial diversity and we by our very presence on the Board of Directors are evidence of that commitment."[35] NOW bylaws reserve a minimum
number of board seats to be occupied by "persons of color." The
NOW Foundation helps fund workshops on prejudice awareness and
sponsored the Women of Color and Allies Summit.

It also "urge[d] the NOW Political Action Committee (PAC) and
all local NOW PACs to withhold endorsement, recommendation, or
support of any kind from any candidate for political office who does
not support affirmative action policies and programs."[36] NOW's by-

laws mandate that subunits create affirmative action plans.[37] In 2001 the group passed a resolution "rededicating ourselves to eliminating racism."[38] Nevertheless, as in all organizations, tensions surface occasionally, perhaps because of the differences that remain between women of color and white women in the way each group frames issues of discrimination and even the concept of feminism.[39] President Kim Gandy announced the appointment of a new Director of Racial Diversity Programs, Zenaida Mendez, an activist with a substantial background in organizing among and for women of color.[40]

The Equal Rights Amendment

NOW's reformulation of the text of the Equal Rights Amendment itself is another example of the organization's radical vision. At its 1995 annual conference NOW delegates passed a resolution supporting another form of the ERA, dubbed the "Constitutional Equality Amendment" (CEA), which specifically protects an individual's civil rights regardless of race, sexual orientation, national origin, or indigence and "guarantees the absolute right of a woman to make her own reproductive decisions including the termination of pregnancy."[41] Controversy erupted at the 2000 annual conference regarding the CEA and the original ERA. A small group of activists working on renewing the ERA campaign wanted a clear statement that NOW delegates unequivocally supported the original ERA. The conference, guided by Patricia Ireland, ultimately passed a resolution worded so as to convey support for both the old and new versions. In this way these activists could return to their states and reassure their coalition partners that NOW backed their participation fully, and national NOW retained the ability to back the expanded version. Far from mollified, however, the ERA activists felt they had received lukewarm support for their cause. This impression is in fact the case: Ireland and national leaders felt that since the passage of any ERA is unlikely, they would rather support the Constitutional Equality Amendment, which more accurately reflects NOW's vanguard vision.

Attention to the question of lesbian and gay rights, as well as the rights of the transgendered, has also figured prominently in NOW's actions, a logical development since lesbians constitute "between 30 and 40 percent of the membership," according to several sources.[42] The organization has been persistently attacked for its perceived hostility to these concerns, despite the fact that the early attempts of NOW's first president, Betty Friedan, to delink feminism and sexuality were soundly rebuffed by members in 1971. Among those expressing frustration at NOW's continued association with the 1971 purge of lesbians in a New York chapter is activist Jan Welch, who became the first elected NOW chapter president as a lesbian in 1971 and was subsequently elected to statewide office in Pennsylvania in 1973.[43] In interviews NOW leaders and members of varying sexual orientation have independently mentioned it as the most irritating misunderstanding about NOW that they encounter.[44] Many lesbian women have served on the national board and as officers. The possibility of discrimination, hostility, exclusion, and misunderstanding still exists, of course, especially at the chapter level. However, with the notable exception of one group of women unhappy with NOW's lack of radicalism in 1975 (a group that subsequently organized NOW's first Lesbian Rights Summit in 1977) and accusations made by a candidate for NOW president in 1992, few complaints of internal insensitivity to lesbian activists and members are found in interviews, organizational documents, or conference records.[45] In addition to conducting frequent workshops on the topic of lesbian rights organizing, in 1994 NOW members included guarantees of lesbian rights in the version of the Constitutional Equality Amendment they endorsed.

NOW frequently finds itself on the cutting edge of the civil rights movement regarding issues of gender and sexuality more generally speaking. For example, at its annual conference in 1997 and again in 2002 NOW members voted to support the rights of the transgendered. NOW's affirmation of the rights of the transgendered seems unlikely to help the organization sidestep controversy or cultivate public support, but it is entirely in keeping with NOW's vanguard, grassroots-oriented governance structure.

Electoral Activism

The hostility to feminist issues on the part of the Republicans since the mid-1980s has made the Democratic Party the "only game in town" for feminists.[46] At the national level the Republican Party expressed disinterest in women's rights issues in the 1990s. A staff member of the Republican National Committee insisted in a 1993 interview that economic issues, not women's issues, mattered to the national Republican Party.[47] EMILY's List reported in 1999 that the future looked no brighter for feminists interested in influencing the Republican agenda: the National Republican Congressional Committee told *Roll Call* that it had "no current plans to try and increase women's participation within the party."[48]

The Democratic Party also earned NOW's ire in the 1990s, however, first in 1992 with its "New Covenant" platform, which supported welfare reform among other conservative policy measures, and again in 1994 as the party scrambled to attract conservative voters by running right-leaning candidates.[49] In 1996 Ireland's speech to the Democratic National Committee criticized the party's proposed addition of a "conscience clause" allowing members to bow out of the party's official position supporting abortion rights; the clause remained in the platform.[50]

With the impetus of the 1996 elections and Newt Gingrich's "Republican revolution," NOW focused on supplying NOW/PAC field organizers to key electoral campaigns to help organize grassroots campaign workers. At NOW's 1996 annual conference, delegates voted to "make electoral politics a major focus for all levels of the organization through November."[51] NOW's newsletter, the *National NOW Times*, noted that "because turnout was low, NOW/PAC's longstanding emphasis on grassroots get-out-the-vote campaigning proved to be a winning strategy for many candidates across the country who succeeded in turning out their strongest supporters."[52] After the 1998 elections NOW/PAC immediately began working on the 2000 campaign cycle, for which it "conducted political trainings and briefings in Washington, D.C., and in the field to enable activists to elect feminist candidates. A network of activists in every congressional district in the country provided NOW/PAC with the nucleus of an effective grassroots political campaign."[53]

For the 1998 congressional elections, NOW/PAC supported eleven successful feminist candidates. The Democratic Party irritated NOW during this election period, having "recruited about a dozen opponents of abortion rights to run for open seats . . . additionally, a number of incumbents, previously steadfast in their support of reproductive rights, have signed on to a bill to ban all late-term abortions."[54] In response, NOW/PAC member Hannah Olanoff emphasized, "As much as we would like to see Newt out of the speaker's chair, we must make it clear that no party has an automatic claim on the feminist vote."[55]

NOW leaders emphasize the group's grassroots contributions to political campaigns. NOW's political action committees are central components of the group's electoral activism. Recognizing the sometimes-fickle nature of politicians' support, NOW/PAC subjects potential recipients of funds to extensive questioning aimed at ensuring that recipients' philosophies match NOW's as closely as possible: "Because NOW's Political Action Committee is the only women's rights PAC that screens candidates on a wide range of feminist issues—full reproductive rights; economic equality; civil rights for all with a strong emphasis on the rights of people of color, lesbians and gay men; affirmative action; and violence against women—none of our endorsed candidates are the kind of people who will waver on women's rights."[56]

Other women's organizations ask for a more limited ideological commitment from candidates seeking their financial support. For example, EMILY's List funnels its bundled contributions to women who are pro-choice Democrats.[57] In the 2000 election cycle the Center for Responsive Politics characterized NOW as a "top donor" in the category of women's issues (ranked fourth). Of thirteen ideological "industries" identified by the center, "women's issues" ranked fourth overall, ahead of "democratic/liberal" donations to candidates.[58] In 1988 NOW was a top contributor in three federal races.[59]

It ranked fourth in the 1998 election cycle, contributing to sixty-three federal candidates and giving more than $58,000 to House candidates.[60] Thirteen PACs categorized as women's-issues PACs contributed to federal candidates in the 2000 election cycle; among them, NOW ranked second in contributions to federal candidates.[61]

NOW leaders and those of other feminist organizations were keenly aware that conservative organizations, including the Christian Coalition, were focusing intently on electoral races at every level of American politics. Formed by Pat Robertson in 1989, the Christian Coalition worked aggressively throughout the 1990s using a combination of grassroots and technologically sophisticated methods to influence national and local political campaigns and referendum issues. The coalition and religious conservatives played an important role in helping Republicans win both houses of Congress in 1994 and succeeded in maintaining a Human Life Amendment plank in the Republican Party platform. In 1996 NOW organized a "Fight the Right" march, which included a focus on the Religious Right's electoral activism, and in a nod to the Christian Coalition's successful voter's guides, NOW/PAC embarked on the creation of an Internet-based Feminist Voter's Guide.[62]

The Christian Coalition stumbled in the late 1990s as it lost the leadership of Ralph Reed, suffered other staff departures, and submitted to investigations into its tax-exempt status by the Internal Revenue Service and the Federal Election Commission. Pat Robertson stepped back in to reorganize, however, launching a $21 million fund-raising drive to elect conservative Christian candidates. For its part, NOW held a three-day "political institute" to train activists in electoral tactics and took what they called an "unprecedented step: asking NOW members to make a monthly pledge to help win back Congress and target key state legislatures. After careful analysis showed antifeminist candidates could capture not only both houses of Congress but also the White House itself, NOW/PAC decided to launch its Victory 2000 Support Committee. The committee's goal is to raise almost a million dollars a month through NOW member pledges to support feminist candidates."[63] In 2002 delegates at NOW's annual conference resolved to "recommend to all NOW

PACs that they make electoral work a priority from now until November and work to elect new feminist candidates to all levels of political office as well as working zealously to bring our incumbent
friends essential reinforcements . . . and recruit and encourage NOW
activists to . . . go to volunteer or work in those targeted fall campaigns."[64]

NOW's enduring commitment to the electoral strategy is clear: an
examination of the workshops presented to national conference attendees since the 1980s shows that national NOW has devoted many
of them to training NOW members to be competent electoral activists; topics regarding general organizing concerns, such as chapter
development, make up the bulk of workshops at conferences (Table
7.1).

Yet, since 1992 NOW has also conducted nonviolent civil disobedience campaigns, fasts, vigils, rallies, "media institutes," boycotts,
and "political institutes" to train electoral organizers. The organization has testified at party platform hearings, held get-out-the-vote
drives, conducted campaigns to alter the media's depiction of
women, run education campaigns such as its "Woman-Friendly
Workplace" campaign, and mobilized demonstrations against such
companies as Mitsubishi and Ford, which were accused of sexual harassment and the unequal treatment of women workers. NOW has
also spoken out against sexist, racist, and homophobic corporations
through its "Merchant of Shame" program. Much of NOW's electoral organizing could not be accomplished without the participation of volunteer activists at the local level, who canvass districts
door to door, hold campaign signs, drop leaflets, and organize get-
out-the-vote drives and rallies.

At the organization's 2003 national conference NOW president
Kim Gandy announced the kickoff of a new campaign: the Drive for
Equality. Like the get-out-the-vote drives NOW had held sporadically
in the past, and the many voter registration campaigns led by organizations on both the left and right, the drive's purpose is to "build an
effective political force to equip activists with the voting tools necessary to motivate women voters to beat George W. Bush."[65]

TABLE 7.1.
Workshops at NOW National Conferences, Selected Years, 1993–2000

Years	General organizing strategies	Media	Young women	Electoral	Reproductive and health	Lesbian	Violence	Poverty
1993 (n-33)	7	1	3	3	5	1	3	3
1997 (n-30)	9	2	1	2	3	2	4	2
1999 (n-26)	9	3	1	3	1	1	0	1
2000 (n-30)	8	2	1	9	2	1	1	2
Total of all workshops (n-119)	33 (26.9%)	8 (6.7%)	6 (5.0%)	17 (14.3%)	11 (9.2%)	5 (4.2%)	8 (6.7%)	8 (6.7%)

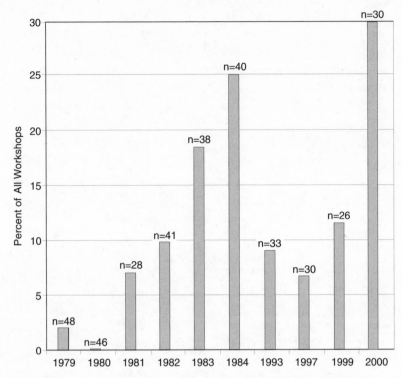

Political action workshops at NOW national conferences, selected years, 1979–2000.

Too Radical or Not Radical Enough? "Family Values" and NOW

Writers, politicians, and pundits have called attention to the inequities engendered by women's dual roles as primary caretakers and wage earners.[66] Some have argued that the feminist movement must reclaim and reframe the "family values" debate that conservatives have used so successfully.[67] In the abstract, such a strategy seems like a winner. It could tap into the needs of many women and men struggling with raising their children and with such burdens as finding good child care, revitalize the women's movement, and mobilize crowds of volunteers unseen since the ERA ratification drive. Securing child care was among NOW's earliest goals and continues to have a place on the group's agenda. Annual conference attendees attended workshops on economic and family security in 2003, which included a discussion of child care issues, for example, and voted to support "family friendly" reforms, such as those called for in a 1999 resolution that declared, "NOW will call for publicly funded, high quality early childhood education and child care programs in all communities." In 2003 NOW leaders claimed that "the federal government is failing today's families," and urged the passage of a comprehensive paid family leave legislation.[68]

Political insiders know one reason NOW would have trouble formulating and implementing a "working-family friendly" strategy: any legislative result would inevitably be a product of compromise. Critics who argue that NOW does not play the legislative game well make an important point. For example, when asked about NOW's involvement in the legislative process, the copresident of the National Women's Law Center acknowledged that the organization's unyielding stands hinder it in this arena: "Legislation is a Herculean feat . . . the compromises required are extraordinary." The president of the Women's Legal Defense Fund concurred, adding that NOW is "impatient with legislating as a strategy."[69]

Why is NOW impatient and uncompromising? Why are other groups less so? As we have seen, NOW's reluctance to compromise and its readiness to antagonize even its allies is practically an organizational hallmark. It has regularly refused to back legislation that contains provisions that violate its goals and values (such as the 1991 Civil Rights Restoration Act, which contained an antiabortion proviso) despite pressure from its allies. NOW's willingness to stand apart, even from progressive allies, is a legacy of its founding commitment to being a vanguard and politically independent organization.

Even if NOW leaders wanted to act as "policy entrepreneurs,"[70] concentrating on family issues by lobbying for the passage of legislation to ease the burden of working parents—seeking the subsidization of child-care centers or increased tax credits, for example—they would have to explain to NOW members why this qualifies as a vanguard issue.[71] It would be much easier for NOW leaders to justify to its internal constituency a piece of legislation calling for universal child care, a more revolutionary concept that the group has called for in the past.

Practically speaking, a more radical piece of legislation, though more palatable to NOW leaders and members, would also be nearly impossible to enact in the United States. Not only would it be a tough sell for fiscally conservative legislators, given the enormous cost of such a policy, but social conservatives would raise major objections as well. And although, as Theda Skocpol argues, universal policies are more palatable to Americans and less likely to become stigmatized, U.S. political culture discourages policy changes that increase the federal government's power.[72] A significant change in federal child-care initiatives may one day be enacted into law. The possibility that NOW would propose, sponsor, or advocate for it if it sought to provide assistance only to "working" families, excluding poor families, the unemployed, legal or illegal immigrants, or minorities, is exceedingly remote.

Major legislative programs demand an enormous investment of time and energy over many years in a very "insider" form of politics, that of legislative lobbying. NOW leaders must justify how they spend their time and NOW members' money. It would be extremely difficult for a NOW leader to defend lobbying for legislation that will result in only incremental change (especially if it is identified as benefiting primarily white, middle-class women) instead of leading campaigns to mobilize and empower the grass roots and supporting issues that, by virtue of being on the cutting edge of feminism, advance feminist consciousness.

Gandy's latest major strategic proposal, the "Drive for Equality," shows how leaders root their initiatives firmly in the organization's political system. In her executive statement she argues that this five-year campaign to influence elections through the ballot box is "the logical next step" for NOW: "Building on NOW's powerful grassroots base, the Drive for Equality will identify, register and mobilize women voters to oust George W. Bush and seek progressive change. To succeed, we will dramatically increase the number and skill level of grassroots activists, build a stronger infrastructure for communication and action, and organize women community by community, campus by campus."[73]

The drive emphasizes "on-the-ground communication with women voters" as well as "empowerment of activists" through trainings. The formal statement outlining the drive's details reflexively asks, "Why NOW?" The answer: "For over thirty-five years, NOW has followed a simple yet profoundly important guiding principle: that organizing at the grass roots—mobilizing individuals to take action—is the single most effective way to create fundamental and lasting social change for women."[74]

The National Organization for Women still hews closely to its guiding principles. In 1998, NOW activists gathered to consider revising the group's 1966 Statement of Purpose. In an interview in 2003, Patricia Ireland noted, "Initially I was very resistant—I became convinced that, even if it didn't come out that much different, we had people in this era who had signed on the dotted line." The "Declaration of Sentiments" that emerged from the meeting noted that, "We are a devoutly grassroots organization. . . . We have sued, boycotted, lobbied, demonstrated, and engaged in nonviolent civil disobedience. . . . We reaffirm our commitment to grassroots activism, to a multi-issue, multi-tactical strategy."[75] Principles are only one component of a group's political system, or governance structure, however. The other component is its set of formal decision-making processes, such as its structure of representation; its bylaws; its financial system; and its procedures for members and leaders to influence policymaking at the national level. In 2003, NOW activists attending the group's annual conference in Arlington, Virginia, had the opportunity to amend the organization's bylaws. A resolution supported by many national NOW leaders proposed to hold membership voting conferences only biennially. Instead, in alternate years NOW would organize issue summits focusing on concerns of progressive activists from the civil rights, disability, lesbian, gay and transgendered, and labor movements as well as members of the public and young feminists. Costly annual voting conferences should be substituted with meetings that reached out to the larger feminist and

progressive community. At the plenary session debating this proposal, NOW President Kim Gandy reassured concerned members
that the national leadership would not act contrary to the membership's will during the intervening years.

Yet this proposed bylaws change, along with all but one that di-
minished activists' power vis-à-vis the national leaders, failed. As
Smeal observed, "Right now there is no grassroots movement for
massive structural change." At an issues hearing debating the amendment to end annual voting conferences, one activist said, "I am a
paper member of lots of organizations but NOW is the one whose
conference I go to. At the first conference I came to, I worked on a
resolution with others, sitting on the floor. It failed, but I felt like I
had participated." About two thirds of the thirty activists attending
the hearing raised their hands when the hearing facilitator asked,
"How many people here have had the experience of working on a
resolution?"[76] In the concluding chapter of this book I use NOW's
2000 annual conference to demonstrate how the "nuts and bolts" of
the organization's decision-making processes provide for a high level
of representation and participation. NOW's decision-making processes transmit the group's guiding principles to new members and
ensure that leaders who stray from these principles must answer to
members.

8. Analyzing Grassroots Representation and Participation

> NOW is excruciatingly democratic.
>
> Kim Gandy

The level of democracy and participation institutionalized in NOW's political system reinforces and reproduces the organization's shared values and goals. Far from serving as "organizational wallpaper," NOW members enjoy access to, and take advantage of, the numerous meaningful opportunities provided by the group's formal decision-making procedures to influence its agenda, structure, and policy positions. At the same time, the high levels of representation and participation constrain the range of possible positions or strategic changes that leaders can legitimately espouse. In other words, NOW's decision-making procedures help ensure that its leaders adhere closely to strategies that reflect the organization's guiding principles.

Decision-Making Processes

NOW's organizational principles and processes stress the grass roots, giving local chapters, states, and regions a great deal of autonomy. Factions within NOW that disagree with local, state, or national leaders' actions can and do use NOW's own organizational infra-

structure and the political skills they learned through NOW to institute reforms. National NOW leaders cannot credibly claim to the
public, to legislators, or to leaders of political parties to have a mass
base if NOW's membership decreases too much, if chapters dwindle
or publicly defy them, or if no one shows up at the demonstrations
they call for. Finally, national leaders regularly face contested elections and may serve for only two consecutive terms.

In most other large voluntary associations a board of directors
nominates and elects the executive officers, but in NOW, members
are charged with this responsibility.[1] NOW's elected officers are a
president, vice president–executive, vice president–action, and vice
president–membership. These salaried officers may serve a maximum of two consecutive four-year terms. They are elected at annual
conferences by delegates, who are chosen in turn by chapters, "with
one delegate for the first ten members and one delegate for each additional thirty members or major fraction thereof." To ensure their
fealty to the organization before they run for office, "all national officers shall have been members of NOW for at least four years immediately prior to election and shall have served at least one year as
a chapter or state officer or National board member," according to
NOW's bylaws. Elections are competitive and involve vigorous (indeed, more than occasionally rancorous) campaigning among the
membership. Including the four elected officers, there are about
thirty paid staff members at the national level. Some states pay their
state presidents a small salary from their share of membership revenue.

Approximately thirty-four members are elected to NOW's board
of directors for a maximum of two consecutive two-year terms. National board elections are held within each of the organization's nine
regions at their respective annual meetings. To increase organizational diversity, NOW's bylaws state that in each region at least one
of the allotted board members' seats must be filled by a "person of
color." (In large regions two seats are reserved for persons of color.)
The national board meets about five times a year. Its members are
unsalaried, although their expenses are reimbursed.

NOW holds its annual conference in a different region each year "for the purpose of transacting the business of the organization." The conference is "the supreme governing body of NOW." It is at these conferences that members elect national leaders, members participate in workshops and issue hearings, special interest caucuses meet, and resolutions are introduced, debated, and voted on. Delegates at issue hearings may vote on any number of proposals, though each hearing may only forward a maximum of two resolutions each, to be voted on by all delegates during the final day of the three-day conference.[2] If activists favor a policy that fails to win support from an issue hearing (or if they want to bypass that process) they can also circulate a petition. Petitions must receive a specified minimum number of signatures of conference attendees, usually between one hundred and two hundred.

One legacy of NOW's founding years is the influence of the women's liberation movement, which insisted on involving the grass roots activists in decision making, thereby empowering them. The moment a group decides to have a group of "leaders" and a group of "followers," however, the possibility arises that the distance thus created will have a negative impact. Concerns about the distance between leaders and members in NOW have sprung up constantly since the group's founding and persist today. A petition circulated at NOW's annual conference in 1993, for example, sought to make officers' salaries equal to those of all other staff members, organizers and receptionists alike. Not only would such a proposal be more consistent with feminist egalitarian principles, some members maintained, but it would also reduce the symbolic distance between leaders and members. Efia Nwangaza, a NOW activist who ran for president in 1993 on a slate opposing Patricia Ireland, argued, "The Ireland administration has maintained an elitist, classist, racist approach to issues . . . typified by Ireland's $110,000 salary and by such recent NOW events as the lebutante ball that was $125 per person [and] the women of power luncheon, which was $100. . . . There was nothing for women who are of average income to make meaningful contact with this organization."[3]

Nwangaza also alleged that the focus of Ireland's team was "not to create a system, to create a world that is inclusive; they just want to be a part of the one that exists." In response, Ireland argued that NOW accommodates lower-income women through sliding-scale membership fees and that Nwangaza underestimated the importance of fund-raising for pursuing NOW's goals. Today these power luncheons, NOW/PAC auctions, and gala dinners continue, annoying many NOW activists who stretch their budgets to attend annual conferences but are then excluded from these events.

Despite complaints like these, NOW leaders are very accessible to members. Officers and board members mingle among activists at national conferences. Board members maintain strong ties to individuals from the state organizations in the regions that elected them and are easily contacted. Individuals are not prevented from joining NOW or participating in its decisions because of a lack of funds; they can register for conferences on a sliding scale, for example. Although it is costly to attend the conferences, which are held in large hotels in major cities around the country, many state organizations raise funds to send some chapter delegates, and activists frequently double and triple up in hotel rooms. States and regions hold smaller-scale events that are both less expensive to attend and more accessible.

NOW leaders, including the four officers and the national board, enjoy a great deal of leverage in shaping national NOW's activity and agenda but much less with respect to the local and state organizations. The officers and board meet independently of the membership at frequent intervals throughout the year and are empowered to make decisions for NOW as a whole between conferences, as long as those decisions are consonant with NOW's Statement of Purpose and bylaws. The board alone holds the power to distribute funds among projects.

Nevertheless, for large projects and changes in policy direction, NOW's officers and its board tend to abstain from action until they have received what amounts to a vote of confidence from activists at annual conferences. For example, leaders conceived and initiated three major electoral projects in the past decade or so, including "Elect Women for a Change," "Victory 2000," and the 2003 "Drive for Equality." Leaders submitted all of these projects to the customary decision-making processes at annual conferences. Members scrutinized, debated, and voted on these proposals twice: once at an issue hearing, where winning majority support allowed the proposals to be placed on the convention's agenda, and then again at a final plenary session.

Ordinary members and chapters also have significant opportunities to influence the organization. First, most chapters have a small core of activists; it is therefore relatively common for committed members to become delegates at NOW's annual convention, chapter officers, state presidents, and regional delegates to the national board within a relatively short time. In addition, NOW chapters are highly autonomous, working only on those national projects that they consider relevant to their sociopolitical environment and their activists' interests. Finally, NOW/PAC endorses only those candidates approved by the state and local organizations.

The Politics of NOW's Policy-Making Process

Analyzing the politics of NOW's resolution process at national conferences demonstrates the balance of power between national NOW and individuals and chapters. Although the specific events described here occurred at NOW's 2000 annual membership conference, I observed similar behavior at every other conference I attended between 1993 and 2003. Throughout NOW's history the organization has engendered a "loyal opposition" within its ranks. In the 1990s a group of individuals from Gainesville, Florida, became regular critics of national NOW. Among other complaints, the Gainesville group claimed that NOW's leaders were ignoring the decline in the number of members and chapters. It also maintained that national NOW's attention was being diverted from pressing issues because of the demands of the NOW Foundation.

The Gainesville contingent initially attempted to garner support for its concerns at the 2000 annual conference by calling for a special constituency caucus. When the activists subsequently convened their own (unauthorized) issue hearing, national officers and board members descended on the gathering, rebutted its claims, and tried to quash the faction's proposals. In the face of national leaders' resistance the group successfully obtained enough signatures by petition to allow two of their proposed resolutions to be placed on the national agenda.

National leaders possess a trump card in the organization's policymaking process: they appoint the members of the Resolutions Committee, which determines the order in which the delegates consider the resolutions. Shortly before commencing its work, one long-standing member of the committee hesitated when questioned about the rules governing its prioritization process. She suggested that resolutions were randomly ordered. However, the next morning the freshly printed agenda listed the Gainesville feminists' resolutions at the bottom of the list, keeping company with a proposal demanding NOW members' commitment to secure women's right to wander "top-free."

The order of resolutions is significant because conference delegates rarely have the opportunity to vote on the latter half of the agenda; time simply runs out. The remainder usually revert to the national board for action, and the board can easily let them fall by the wayside. The Gainesville faction, although mostly young feminists, used Robert's Rules of Order with aplomb, their strategies gleaned from supportive NOW leaders in their state and region. Employing parliamentary procedures, they attempted to reposition their resolutions and, when that failed, to hasten the debate on other proposals in the hope that their resolutions might be considered before the conference deconvened.[4]

Ultimately, their maneuvers did not succeed. Nevertheless, the mobilization of factions like this one reinforces national NOW's accountability. As members of a "loyal opposition," these activists also remind other, perhaps more jaded or less knowledgeable members about NOW's principles and vision. Bringing these issues to light helps ensure that NOW leaders carry out their obligations to the membership.

Individual NOW members can effect change in the national organization without the immediate consent of national leaders, especially when activists are persistent, patient, and willing and able to mobilize others. In 1995 a faction calling itself the "Nyack Group" and voicing concern about NOW's lack of focus, argued that the organization must conduct strategic planning. This proposal failed, but as a compromise, former board member Gay Bruhn suggested to the national board the idea of holding a national conference that would reconsider NOW's purpose—a "Vision Summit." The board demurred, but Bruhn persisted, ultimately succeeding in winning support to hold the summit at the 1998 annual conference.

Active members greatly influence the efficacy of the entire organization. For example, approved conference resolutions are referred to Conference Implementation Committees (CICs), whose members are appointed by NOW's president with the advice and consent of the board. If the chair of the CIC devoted to the resolution to update NOW's consciousness-raising manual, for example, does not persevere by contacting the other members, setting up meetings, and following up on tasks, the manual does not get revised. The distance between regions presents a constant challenge, making it difficult for committees to meet easily, and financial (CICs have a small budget) and time pressures threaten the implementation of even those resolutions passed by "the supreme governing body of NOW" in the absence of member participation.

Civic Skills and Civic Education

Mediating institutions, as Harry Boyte observes, are one mechanism through which civic skills are imparted to citizens. They constitute "settings grounded in everyday life and reaching into arenas of policy and large institutions where people learn to act with political savvy."[5] According to Louis Ayala, civic skills are "the participatory or 'democratic' type activities which [organizations] give their members the opportunity to perform, and which are supposed to increase the likelihood of these same members participating in the political process."[6] Participating in voluntary associations may encourage members to become more widely active in national politics as well:

as Verba, Schlozman, and Brady suggest, these skills are transferable to other venues.[7]

In many ways NOW is a "school for democracy." Both leaders and rank-and-file members teach and wield the political skills that are necessary to function effectively not only in other interest groups but also in formal political institutions, from school boards to legislatures. Among the competencies NOW members attain are the (strategic) use of parliamentary procedure, an understanding of legislative processes at all governmental levels (including not only lobbying tactics but also policy formation and implementation), and exposure to the mechanics of local, state, and national electoral politics, such as how to develop campaigns to inform or mobilize citizens in anticipation of elections.

Sponsoring Democratic Deliberation

NOW's governance system contributes to members' engagement in the organization and, potentially, in the larger political world in at least two consequential ways. First, the organization transmits civic skills to members. Second, NOW hosts the "face-to-face" encounters scholars argue are so critical to the development of social capital and to a genuine and democratic public sphere in which deliberative decision making may flourish.

Pamela Paxton notes that the quality of citizen participation, rather than the sheer number of political acts, should concern scholars interested in the relationship between civic engagement and democracy.[8] The quality of citizens' engagement may be measured in part by probing the extent to which individuals are provided occasions to exchange viewpoints with others in the associations to which they belong. Scholars have argued in fact that a significant fraction of citizen participation must be devoted to discursive acts, preferably in open forums that grant participants significant freedom of expression. Sara Evans and Harry Boyte term these forums "free spaces"; Jürgen Habermas envisions a "public sphere," "a discursive arena that is home to citizen debate, deliberation, agreement and action."[9] Similarly, Kevin Mattson proposes the establishment of "democratic publics," which represent an authentic, deliberative politics.[10]

Regardless of the specific term employed, those postulating the need for a more deliberative politics contend that venues that encourage face-to-face interactions and free exchanges among citizens produce and sustain a more vigorous and democratic polity.[11] Jane Mansbridge claims, for example, that such deliberation can induce citizens to become committed to pursuing common goals and interests.[12] For Benjamin Barber, these forms of public communication are also valuable because they are more egalitarian than other types of political discourse.[13]

The governance structure of the National Organization for Women provides members with regular opportunities and "free space" in which to debate, discuss, disagree, and finally come to agreement with other members. NOW members are regularly exposed to new ways of thinking about their own lives, their communities, and the nation.[14] Occasionally, NOW leaders resort to the manipulative tactics that C. Wright Mills argues are often deployed by those in authority to suppress policies they oppose.[15] Nevertheless, it is clear that NOW's structure offers members frequent opportunities to join, initiate, and direct meaningful discussions about policies and problems that concern them. Members enjoy significant autonomy from national leaders, including the freedom of public dissent at NOW-sponsored gatherings. The democratic deliberations that occur within NOW encourage member-citizens to adopt less self-interested points of view.[16] Finally, by organizing summits aimed at nonmembers, NOW frequently reaches out with the kind of "bridging" activities that Robert Putnam believes enhance civic engagement.[17]

An important contrast to the positive cast of these activities is the fact that, as in any large voluntary organization, the majority of NOW members devote a minimal amount of time and attention to the organization, limiting their participation to making an annual financial contribution. Rather than dismiss these individuals, we can characterize them more accurately as a cohort of "latent" members: individuals who could be "activated" but who are not currently involved in substantial ways.[18] Yet, politically salient issues have the potential to draw these members into more active civic participation.

Voluntary associations can translate the energy of newly activated members into political power. Interest groups such as the National Organization for Women offer multiple channels for converting latent members into knowledgeable and competent participants in civic life. For example, NOW incorporated thousands of new activists during the campaign to ratify the Equal Rights Amendment between 1972 and 1982. The organization's structure, networks, and information production dramatically lowers the costs of information and participation for all members, latent and active alike. When a personal or political condition arouses their activism, latent members benefit from the organization's infrastructure.[19]

NOW may not be typical of the groups active in politics today. Yet other research suggests that it is not alone in fostering civic engagement.[20] Large national organizations such as the Sierra Club also encourage and subsidize gatherings devoted to public deliberation and the development of transferable civic skills. Even AARP, whose board amended its bylaws, thereby removing virtually all institutionalized methods by which members can influence the national level's priorities, finds itself threatened by the possibility that its members might abandon it. In addition, AARP depends on the participation of thousands of volunteers each day for the maintenance of its programs.

Similarly, in a large study of peace movement organizations, Bob Edwards and Michael Foley found that "between 20% and 28% of national groups do involve members in elections and participation in decision-making, and that some 60% of them claim to have members working directly on peace issues . . . in contrast to the contentions of recent critics of advocacy groups, the majority of groups, including many national ones, involve their members directly in working on issues (60%), recruiting new members (52%), and fund raising (48%)."[21] Edwards and Foley find that "only 12% of national SMOs [social movement organizations] fit the much maligned 'checkbook membership' characterization and are no more likely to do so than most other SMOs."[22] John D. McCarthy and Mark Wolfson's analysis of Mothers Against Drunk Driving (MADD) confirms that an organization's structure, particularly when it provides for substantial autonomy for members or chapters, increases substantive participation among them.[23]

Conclusion

Voluntary associations do not require a democratic, progressive governance structure in order to pursue their goals successfully. Groups can be resolutely undemocratic and yet highly effective. In this book I do not mean to suggest that NOW's principles and practices constitute either an organizational ideal.

Rather, I want to suggest the resuscitation of an approach to analyzing group politics that has been employed productively by earlier scholars of parties and interest groups (perhaps most memorably in Michels's analysis of political party structure and Lipset, Trow, and Coleman's study of the inner workings of a labor union)[24] and more recently by political scientists interested in explaining the political development of nations.[25] In teasing out why the United States has adopted certain social policies and not others, for example, scholars have begun to look not only at resources and political context—though these are undeniably crucial variables—but also at how polity members' lived experiences and values became incorporated into decision-making structures.

The same framework can be employed to understand the historical behavior and predict the future behavior of voluntary associations. Groups' internal political structures incorporate founders' values and policy-making rules. A group's subsequent decisions about the strategies it employs and the ones it automatically rejects, the alliances it forms and those it shuns—depend on the particular governance structure it has institutionalized. With enough information about the governance structures of individual social movement groups, we may be able to predict the future mobilizing capacity not only of those organizations but also of social movements more broadly.

Notes

Preface

1. See Robert Michels, *Political Parties* (New York: Free Press, 1915/1958); E.E. Schattschneider, *Politics, Pressure, and the Tariff: A Study of Free Private Enterprise in Pressure Politics* (Hamden, Conn.: Archon Books, 1935/1963); Moisei Ostrogorski and Seymour M. Lipset, *Democracy and the Organization of Political Parties* (New Brunswick, N.J.: Transaction Press, 1970); and Seymour Martin Lipset, Martin A. Trow, and James S. Coleman, *Union Democracy: The Internal Politics of the International Typographical Union* (New York: Free Press, 1956).

2. Jane Mansbridge, *Why We Lost the ERA* (Chicago: University of Chicago Press, 1986).

3. All primary documents, unless noted otherwise, are archived at the Schlesinger Library, Radcliffe College, Harvard University, National Organization for Women Collection.

4. For a detailed explanation, see Michael Huberman and Matthew B. Miles, *Qualitative Data Analysis: An Expanded Sourcebook*, 2d ed. (Thousand Oaks, Calif.: Sage, 1994).

1. Governance Structures and Strategy Choice and Change in Membership Organizations

1. Scholars of the feminist movement have been more consistently sensitive than others to internal group politics. See Jo Freeman, *The Politics of Women's Liberation: A Case Study of an Emerging Social Movement and Its Relation to the Policy Process* (New York: David McKay, 1975); Barbara Ryan, *Feminism and the Women's Movement: Dynamics of Change in Social Movement Ideology and Activism* (New York: Routledge, 1992); Wini Breines, *Community and Organization in the New Left,*

1962–1968 (New York: Praeger, 1982); Myra Marx Ferree and Beth B. Hess, *Controversy and Coalition: The New Feminist Movement* (Boston: Twayne, 1985); Sara Evans, *Personal Politics: The Roots of Women's Liberation in the Civil Rights Movement and the New Left* (New York: Random House, 1979); Suzanne Staggenborg, *The Pro-Choice Movement: Organization and Activism in the Abortion Conflict* (New York: Oxford University Press, 1991); Jo Reger, "Social Movement Culture and Organizational Survival in the National Organization for Women," Ph.D. diss., Ohio State University, 1997.

2. Observers noting this dearth include Jeffrey Berry, "An Agenda for Research on Interest Groups," in *Representing Interests and Interest Group Representation*, ed. William Crotty, Mildred A. Schwartz, and John C. Green (Lanham, Md.: University Press of America, 1994), 22; C. Coglianese, "Unequal Representation: Membership Input and Interest Group Decision-Making," 1996, http://www.ksg.harvard.edu/prg/cary/unequal.htm. Some important exceptions among political scientists include Andrew S. McFarland, *Common Cause: Lobbying in the Public Interest* (Chatham, N.J.: Chatham House, 1984), and Lawrence S. Rothenberg, *From the Ground Up: Linking Citizens to Politics at Common Cause* (Cambridge: Cambridge University Press, 1992). See also Kay Lehman Schlozman and John T. Tierney, *Organized Interests and American Democracy* (New York: Harper & Row, 1986).

3. Jack L. Walker Jr., *Mobilizing Interest Groups in America: Patrons, Professions, and Social Movements* (Ann Arbor: University of Michigan Press, 1991); Robert H. Salisbury, "An Exchange Theory of Interest Groups," *Midwest Journal of Political Science* 13 (1969): 1–13; Terry Moe, "Toward a Broader View of Interest Groups," *Journal of Politics* 43 (1981): 531–43.

4. John D. McCarthy and Mayer N. Zald, "Resource Mobilization and Social Movements: A Partial Theory," *American Journal of Sociology* 82 (1977): 1212–41, and McCarthy and Zald, *Social Movements in an Organizational Society* (New Brunswick, N.J.: Transaction, 1987), describe classic resource mobilization theory. For critiques, see Douglas McAdam, *The Political Process and the Development of Black Insurgency, 1930–1970* (Chicago: University of Chicago Press, 1982). On the role of patrons, see Walker, *Mobilizing Interest Groups*; Frank Baumgartner and Beth Leech, *Basic Interests: The Importance of Groups in Politics and Political Science* (Princeton: Princeton University Press, 1998), 12; and the following extended debate: Anthony J. Nownes and Grant Neeley, "Public Interest Group Entrepreneurship and Theories of Group Mobilization," *Political Research Quarterly* 1 (1996): 119–46; Douglas R. Imig and Jeffrey M. Berry, "Patrons and Entrepreneurs: A Response to 'Public Interest Group Entrepreneurship and Theories of Group Mobilization,'" *Political Research Quarterly* 1 (1996): 147–54; Anthony J. Nownes, "Response to Imig and Berry: Entrepreneurs, Patrons, and Organization," *Political Research Quarterly* 1 (1996): 155–62.

5. Peter K. Eisinger, "The Conditions of Protest Behavior in American Cities," *American Political Science Review* 67 (1973):11–28; McAdam, *Political Process*; Aldon D. Morris, *The Origins of the Civil Rights Movement* (New York: Free Press, 1984); Freeman, *Politics of Women's Liberation*; Anne N. Costain, *Inviting Women's Rebellion: A Political Process Interpretation of the Women's Movement* (Baltimore: Johns Hopkins University Press, 1992); Anthony Oberschall, *Social Conflict and Social Movements* (Englewood Cliffs, N.J.: Prentice-Hall, 1973).

6. McAdam, *Political Process*.

7. See Andrew S. McFarland, *Common Cause: Lobbying in the Public Interest* (Chatham, N.J.: Chatham House, 1984); Lee Ann Banaszak, *Why Movements Succeed or Fail: Opportunity, Culture, and the Struggle for Woman Suffrage* (Princeton:

Princeton University Press, 1996); Elisabeth Clemens, "Organizational Form as Frame: Collective Identity and Political Strategy in the American Labor Movement, 1880–1920," in *Comparative Perspectives on Social Movements: Political Opportunities, Mobilizing Structures, and Cultural Framings*, ed. Doug McAdam, John D. McCarthy, and Mayer N. Zald (Cambridge: Cambridge University Press, 1996); Elisabeth S. Clemens, *The People's Lobby: Organizational Innovation and the Rise of Interest Group Politics in the United States, 1890–1925* (Chicago: Chicago University Press, 1997); Ronald G. Shaiko, *Voices and Echoes for the Environment* (New York: Columbia University Press, 1999); Debra C. Minkoff, "Walking a Political Tightrope: Responsiveness and Internal Accountability in Social Movement Organizations," *Governance and Accountability: Nonprofit Advocacy and the Policy Process*, issue 2 in the series "Exploring Organizations and Advocacy," ed. Elizabeth Reid and Maria D. Montilla (fall/winter 2000–2001), http://www.urban.org/url.cfm?ID=410532.

8. Clemens, *The People's Lobby*.

9. Alice Echols, *Daring To Be Bad: Radical Feminism in America, 1967–1975* (Minneapolis: University of Minnesota Press, 1989).

10. Douglas McAdam, Sidney Tarrow, and Charles Tilly, "To Map Contentious Politics," *Mobilization* 1 (1996): 23.

11. Marshall Ganz, "Resources and Resourcefulness: Leadership, Strategy, and Organization in the Unionization of California Agriculture (1959–1966)," *American Journal of Sociology* 105 (2000).

12. Ganz, "Resources and Resourcefulness"; Bert Klandermans, "Mobilization and Participation: Social Psychological Expansions of Resource Mobilization Theory," *American Sociological Review* 49 (1984): 583–600; Debra Friedman and Douglas McAdam, "Collective Identity and Activism: Networks, Choices, and the Life of a Social Movement," in *Frontiers in Social Movement Theory*, ed. Aldon D. Morris and Carol McClurg Mueller (New Haven: Yale University Press, 1992); William Gamson, *The Strategy of Social Protest* (Homewood, Ill.: Dorsey Press, 1975/1990); Lee Ann Banaszak, *Why Movements Succeed or Fail: Opportunity, Culture, and the Struggle for Woman Suffrage* (Princeton: Princeton University Press, 1996).

13. David Knoke, *Organizing for Collective Action: The Political Economies of Associations* (Hawthorne, N.Y.: Aldine de Gruyter, 1990), 159.

14. Knoke, *Organizing for Collective Action:* The Political Economies of Associations (Hawthorne, N.Y.: Aldine de Gruyter, 1990), 160.

15. Steven E. Schier, *By Invitation Only: The Rise of Exclusive Politics in the United States* (Pittsburgh: University of Pittsburgh Press, 2000); Theda Skocpol, "Advocates without Members: The Recent Transformation of Associational Life," in *Civic Engagement in American Democracy*, ed. Theda Skocpol and Morris P. Fiorina (Washington, D.C.: Brookings Institution Press, 1999), 461–510; Robert D. Putnam, *Bowling Alone: The Collapse and Revival of American Community* (New York: Touchstone, 2000); John B. Judis, "The Pressure Elite: Inside the Narrow World of Advocacy Group Politics," *American Prospect* 3 (1992): 15–19; Jack L. Walker, "The Origins and Maintenance of Interest Groups in America," *American Political Science Review* 77 (1983): 390–406.

16. Sidney Verba, Kay Lehman Schlozman, and Henry E. Brady, *Voice and Equality: Civic Voluntarism in American Politics* (Cambridge, Mass.: Belknap Press, 1995). See also Baumgartner and Leech, *Basic Interests*.

17. Martha L. McCoy and Patrick L. Scully, "Deliberative Dialogue to Expand Civic Engagement: What Kind of Talk Does Democracy Need?" *National Civic Review* (2002): 118.

18. Harry C. Boyte, "On Silences and Civic Muscle, or Why Social Capital Is a

Useful but Insufficient Concept," paper presented at the Havens Center, University of Wisconsin-Madison, April 10, 2001.

19. See, for example, Verba, Schlozman, and Brady, *Voice and Equality*; Putnam, *Bowling Alone*; Jocelyn Elise Crowley and Theda Skocpol, "The Rush to Organize: Explaining Associational Formation in the United States, 1960–1920," *American Journal of Political Science* 45 (2001): 813–29; James E. Curtis, Douglas E. Baer, and Edward C. Grabb, "Nations of Joiners: Voluntary Association Membership in Democratic Societies," *American Sociological Review* 66 (2001): 783–805; Pamela Paxton, "Social Capital and Democracy: An Interdependent Relationship," *American Sociological Review* 67 (2002): 254–77; Richard A. Couto with Catherine S. Guthrie, *Making Democracy Work Better: Mediating Structures, Social Capital, and the Democratic Prospect* (Chapel Hill: University of North Carolina Press, 1999).

20. Sidney Verba, Norman Nie, and Jae-On Kim, *Participation and Political Equality: A Cross-National Comparison* (Cambridge: Cambridge University Press, 1978); Verba, Schlozman, and Brady, *Voice and Equality*; Raymond E. Wolfinger and Steven J. Rosenstone, *Who Votes?* (New Haven: Yale University Press, 1980); Robert D. Putnam with R. Leonardi and R. Y. Nanetti, *Making Democracy Work: Civic Traditions in Modern Italy* (Princeton: Princeton University Press, 1993).

21. Verba, Schlozman, and Brady, *Voice and Equality*, 313.

2. Inventing NOW

1. Arthur L. Stinchcombe, *Constructing Social Theories* (Chicago: University of Chicago Press, 1968).

2. "Powell Urges Negroes to Work toward 'Black Political Power,' " *New York Times*, July 30, 1966.

3. I use the term *chairman* when it was employed by the individuals concerned at the time.

4. NOW, Statement of Purpose, 1966.

5. Jo Freeman, *The Politics of Women's Liberation: A Case Study of an Emerging Social Movement and Its Relation to the Policy Process* (New York: David McKay, 1975), 80–86, confirms NOW's increasing radicalization.

6. On the way these experiences may influence future mobilizations, see, for example, Douglas McAdam, *The Political Process and the Development of Black Insurgency, 1930–1970* (Chicago: University of Chicago Press, 1982); Verta Taylor, "Social Movement Continuity: The Women's Movement in Abeyance," *American Sociological Review* 54 (1989): 761–75.

7. Lee Graham, "Who's in Charge Here? Not Women!" *New York Times*, September 2, 1962.

8. "Women Likely to Outvote Men," *New York Times*, January 5, 1960; "Backs Women's Rights: Nixon Favors Amendment to Guarantee Sex Equality," *New York Times*, September 3, 1960; "A Chivalrous Kennedy Backs Women's Rights," *New York Times*, November 9, 1961. Also see President Richard M. Nixon's speech to delegates to the Girls Nation Annual Convention, August 6, 1971, Public Papers of the Presidents of the United States, Richard Nixon (Washington, D.C.: Government Printing Office, 1972).

9. "An Invitation to Join" (1966).

10. Letter from President Betty Friedan to Member of Board of Directors Alice Rossi (October 20, 1967). See also Sara Evans, *Personal Politics: The Roots of Women's Liberation in the Civil Rights Movement and the New Left* (New York: Random House, 1979).

11. Leila J. Rupp and Verta Taylor, *Survival in the Doldrums: the American Women's Rights Movement, 1954 to the 1960s* (New York: Oxford University Press, 1987); Evans, *Personal Politics*; Freeman, *Politics of Women's Liberation*; Judith Hole and Ellen Levine, *Rebirth of Feminism* (New York: Quadrangle/New York Times, 1971); Ethel Klein, *Gender Politics: From Consciousness to Mass Politics* (Cambridge: Harvard University Press, 1984).

12. A. H. Raskin, "Negro Labor Unit Names 2 Women," *New York Times*, May 30, 1960.

13. "Observer," *New York Times*, December 15, 1962.

14. Fred Powledge, "Who Leads the Negro? Civil Rights Leaders Ask Themselves More and More Searching Questions," *New York Times*, January 13, 1964.

15. Powledge, "Who Leads the Negro?"

16. Austin C. Wehrwein, "252 Protesters Held in Chicago," *New York Times*, June 12, 1965.

17. Daniel Bell, "Plea for a 'New Phase in Negro Leadership,'" *New York Times*, May 31, 1964; M. S. Handler, "N.A.A.C.P. Keeps Moderate View," *New York Times*, June 24, 1964.

18. M. S. Handler, "Mississippi Faces Drive for Rights," *New York Times*, May 17, 1964.

19. Paul I. Montgomery, "45 Negro Leaders Outline '65 Aims," *New York Times*, February 1, 1965.

20. The director of the Department of Labor's Women's Bureau played a significant role in bringing about these early conferences. "Women to Review Gains," *New York Times*, February 6, 1948.

21. Bess Furman, "Truman Bids Women Use Purse in Fight on High Cost of Living," *New York Times*, February 18, 1948.

22. Graham, "Who's in Charge Here?"

23. Sal Nuccio, "Personal Finance: On Women's Rights," *New York Times*, August 22, 1966.

24. "U.N. Finds 47 Countries Uphold Women's Rights," *New York Times*, December 26, 1947.

25. "Women's Rights Pact in Force Wednesday," *New York Times*, July 5, 1954.

26. "Gain in Women's Cause," *New York Times*, December 22, 1952; "U.N. Study Scheduled on Women's Rights," *New York Times*, January 22, 1953.

27. "Celler Pushes Bill on Women's Rights," *New York Times*, February 15, 1953.

28. Alvin Shuster, "President Names Panel on Women," *New York Times*, December 15, 1961.

29. John Herbers, "Women Complain of Bias on Jobs," *New York Times*, July 27, 1965.

30. Agnes McCarty, "300 Women Meet at Yale on Life Role," *New York Times*, June 14, 1956.

31. Richard H. Parkes, "Norwalk Groups Retort to Mayor," *New York Times*, June 13, 1959.

32. "News Guild Urges Equal Job Status," *New York Times*, July 13, 1962.

33. Jo Freeman, *A Room at a Time: How Women Entered Party Politics* (Lanham, Md.: Rowman & Littlefield, 2000).

34. "Women Elect Leader," *New York Times*, January 7, 1960.

35. Marylin Bender, "Woman Is Beginning to Find Her Place—and It's Not in the Kitchen," *New York Times*, February 16, 1966.

36. Bender, "Woman Is Beginning."

37. Toni Carabillo, Judith Meuli, and June Bundy Csida, *Feminist Chronicles* (Los Angeles: Women's Graphics, 1993), 47.

38. Joan Cook, " 'Mystique' View Backed by Many, Author Finds," *New York Times*, March 12, 1964. Betty Friedan, *The Feminist Mystique* (New York: W. W. Norton, 1963).

39. Flora Davis, *Moving the Mountain: The Women's Movement in America since 1960* (Urbana: University of Illinois Press, 1999); Betty Friedan, *Life So Far* (New York: Simon and Schuster, 2000).

40. Friedan, *Life So Far*, 169.

41. Davis, *Moving the Mountain*, 54.

42. Davis, *Moving the Mountain*, 54.

43. "Minutes of the Organizing Conference," October 1966.

44. "Report of the Legal Committee to Board and Members of NOW at First Annual Conference," November 1967.

45. Jo Freeman, "A Model for Analyzing the Strategic Options of Social Movement Organizations," in *Waves of Protest: Social Movements since the 1960s*, ed. Jo Freeman and Victoria Johnson (Lanham, Md.: Rowman & Littlefield, 1999), 223.

46. Friedan, *Life So Far*, 184.

47. Freeman, *The Politics of Liberation*; Ferree and Hess, *Controversy and Coalition*, 57–64. See also Redstockings of the Women's Liberation Movement, *Feminist Revolution: An Abridged Edition with Additional Writings* (New York: Random House, 1975/1978); Alice Echols, *Daring to Be Bad: Radical Feminism in America, 1967–1975* (Minneapolis: University of Minnesota Press, 1989); and the documentary reader Barbara A. Crow, ed., *Radical Feminism* (New York: New York University Press, 2000).

48. Wini Breines, *Community and Organization in the New Left, 1962–1968* (New York: Praeger, 1982), 6.

49. Carabillo, Meuli, and Csida, *Feminist Chronicles*, 159.

50. Carabillo, Meuli, and Csida, *Feminist Chronicles*, 163.

51. Friedan, *Life So Far*, 171. Emphasis in original. Perhaps she was aware of incidents such as the suspension by Roy Wilkins, executive secretary of the NAACP, of the president of a North Carolina chapter for "having urged Negroes 'to meet violence with violence.' " "N.A.A.C.P. Unit Leader Fights His Suspension," *New York Times*, May 8, 1959.

52. M. S. Handler, "N.A.A.C.P. Keeps Moderate View," *New York Times*, June 24, 1964. See also, Handler, "Negro Protests Held Effective," *New York Times*, June 15, 1964.

53. Dolores Alexander, "An Editorial: The Women's Movement: A Unique Revolution Demanding a Unique Ideology for NOW," *NOW ACTS*, 1969.

54. "Invitation to Join," in Carabillo, Meuli, and Csida, *Feminist Chronicles*, 164.

55. "Statement of Purpose," in Carabillo, Meuli, and Csida, *Feminist Chronicles*, 159.

56. "Statement of Purpose," in Carabillo, Meuli, and Csida, *Feminist Chronicles*, 159.

57. Report by Betty Friedan, President, to All Members of NOW, January 15, 1968, in Carabillo, Meuli, and Csida, *Feminist Chronicles*, 180–81.

58. Rupp and Taylor, *Survival in the Doldrums*, 148.

59. Raskin, "Negro Labor Unit."

60. Lisa Hammel, "They Met in Victorian Parlor to Demand 'True Equality'— NOW," *New York Times*, November 22, 1966.

61. Letter from Alice Rossi to potential members, September 1966.

62. "Key Negro Leaders Ask Curbs on Protests till after Election," *New York Times*, July 30, 1964.

63. Rupp and Taylor, *Survival in the Doldrums*, 203.

64. Rupp and Taylor, *Survival in the Doldrums*, 203–4.

65. NOW Statement of Purpose, 1966.

66. Letter to Betty Friedan from Alice Rossi, August 23, 1966.

67. Letter from Betty Friedan to Alice Rossi, October 12, 1966.

68. Freeman, *Politics of Women's Liberation*, 119–29; Hole and Levine, *Rebirth of Feminism*, 159–63; Carol McClurg Mueller, "The Organizational Basis of Conflict in Contemporary Feminism," in *Feminist Organizations: Harvest of the New Women's Movement*, ed. Myra Marx Ferree and Patricia Yancey Martin (Philadelphia: Temple University Press, 1995), 271–72; Suzanne Staggenborg, *The Pro-Choice Movement: Organization and Activism in the Abortion Conflict* (New York: Oxford University Press, 1991).

69. Jo Freeman, "From Seed to Harvest: Transformations of Feminist Organizations and Scholarship," in *Feminist Organizations: Harvest of the New Women's Movement*, ed. Myra Marx Ferree and Patricia Yancey Martin (Philadelphia: Temple University Press, 1995), 407–8.

70. Minutes of the Organizing Conference, October 29, 1966.

71. Freeman, "Model," 232.

72. Report of the President, National Board Meeting Minutes, December 6, 1969.

73. Susan Brownmiller, "Sisterhood Is Powerful," *New York Times*, March 15, 1970.

74. Report of the President, National Board Meeting Minutes, December 6, 1969.

75. Report of the President, National Board Meeting Minutes, December 6, 1969.

76. Report of the President, National Board Meeting Minutes, December 6, 1969.

77. Minutes of the Organizing Conference, October 29, 1966.

78. These numbers soon exploded, and by 1972 there were two hundred chapters. Friedan, *Life so Far*, 232; Carabillo, Meuli, and Csida, *Feminist Chronicles*, 61.

79. Freeman, *Politics of Women's Liberation*, 88.

80. Freeman, *Politics of Women's Liberation*, 87.

81. Letter to Kathryn Clarenbach from Alice S. Rossi, November 9, 1966.

82. Report of Informal Meeting of NOW Members from Illinois, Indiana, and Wisconsin, January 21, 1967.

83. Report of Informal Meeting of NOW Members from Illinois, Indiana, and Wisconsin, January 21, 1967.

84. Memo to Board of Directors from Kathryn F. Clarenbach, June 14, 1967.

85. Freeman, *Politics of Women's Liberation*, 91.

86. Minutes, National Board Meeting, November 27–28, 1968, 9.

87. Minutes, National Board Meeting, November 27–28, 1968, 3.

88. *NOW ACTS*, March 1969.

89. Minutes, National Board Meeting, December 6, 1969.

90. Minutes, National Board Meeting, December 6, 1969.

91. "Dollars and Sense of Revolution," *NOW ACTS*, winter 1970.

92. *NOW ACTS*, March 1969.

93. "Dollars and Sense."

94. Memo to all board members from Betty Friedan, January 24, 1967.

95. Today NOW has nine regions.

3. NOW's Strategic Evolution

1. Letter from President Betty Friedan to Alice Rossi, September 20, 1967.

2. Report of Informal Meeting of NOW members from Illinois, Indiana, and Wisconsin, 1967.

3. Letter from Alice S. Rossi to Dr. Kathryn F. Clarenbach, October 4, 1966.

4. Letter from Rossi to Clarenbach, October 4, 1966.

5. Letter from Alice S. Rossi to Dr. Kathryn F. Clarenbach, December 13, 1966.

6. Memo to All Board Members from NOW President Friedan, January 24, 1967.

7. Friedan, *Life So Far*, 177.

8. Freeman, "Model," 223.

9. Janet A. Flammang, *Women's Political Voice: How Women Are Transforming the Practice and Study of Politics* (Philadelphia: Temple University Press, 1997), 84.

10. *New York Times*, April 5, 1970.

11. Sidney Tarrow, *Power in Movement: Collective Action, Social Movements, and Politics* (Cambridge: Cambridge University Press, 1994).

12. Freeman, *The Politics of Women's Liberation*; Frances Fox Piven and Richard Cloward, *Poor People's Movements: Why They Succeed, How They Fail* (New York: Vintage, 1977/1979); Suzanne Staggenborg, "The Consequences of Professionalization and Formalization in the Pro-Choice Movement," *American Sociological Review* 53 (1988): 585–605. Also see Anne N. Costain and W. Douglas Costain, "Strategy and Tactics of the Women's Movement in the United States: The Role of Political Parties," in *The Women's Movements of the United States and Western Europe*, ed. Mary Fainsod Katzenstein and Carol McClurg Mueller (Philadelphia: Temple University Press, 1987), 204.

13. Carabillo, Meuli, and Csida, *Feminist Chronicles*, 178.

14. Carabillo, Meuli, and Csida, *Feminist Chronicles*, 47.

15. Freeman, "Model," 230.

16. "11 Picket Times Classified Office to Protest Male-Female Labels," *New York Times*, August 31, 1967; Marylin Bender, "The Feminists Are on the March Once More," *New York Times*, December 14, 1967.

17. Charlotte Curtis, "White House Candidates Let Women Down," *New York Times*, May 7, 1968.

18. "Woman Crusaders Test Plaza's 'Men Only' Rule," *New York Times*, February 13, 1969; Grace Lichtenstein, "McSorley's Admits Women under a New City Law," *New York Times*, August 11, 1970.

19. Deidre Carmody, " General Strike by U.S. Woman Urged to Mark 19th Amendment," *New York Times*, March 21, 1970.

20. National Board Meeting Minutes, March 29–30, 1969.

21. National Board Meeting Minutes, March 29–30, 1969.

22. National Board Meeting Minutes, May 2–3, 1970.

23. National Board Meeting Minutes, May 2–3, 1970.

24. "Women Open Political Series," *New York Times*, July 18, 1971.

25. "Task Forces, Politics '71'76," folder.

26. "NOW Politics Task Force Report," October 1972.

27. Flammang, *Women's Political Voice*, 84.

28. "Revolution: Tomorrow Is NOW" (1972–73?); "Summary of Questionnaire for NOW," 1974.

29. "NOW Conferences Make History," Natl. NOW Conference Book, 1979, 8.

30. "National Organization for Women Policy Manual: Issues," 1979, 69.

31. "Chapter News," *NOW ACTS*, May 1968.

32. Report, President Friedan, Minutes of Natl. Board Meeting, June 28–29, 1969.

33. Report, President Friedan, Minutes of National Board Meeting, June 28–29, 1969.

34. Linda Greenhouse, "Women's Groups Pressing Reforms," *New York Times*, November 25, 1969.

35. Report, President Friedan, Minutes of National Board Meeting, December 6, 1969.

36. *New York Times*, July 26, 1970.

37. *New York Times*, September 12, 1971.

38. "Highlights of NOW's National Membership Conference, December 7–8, 1968 in Atlanta," *NOW ACTS*, February 1969. Also in this issue see Alexander, "An Editorial."

39. Martha Weijnman Lear, "What Do These Women *Want*? The Second Feminist Wave," March 10, 1968, *New York Times*.

40. Freeman, *Politics of Women's Liberation*, 86.

41. Memo to Board of Directors from Kathryn F. Clarenbach, June 14, 1967.

42. Kathie Sarachild, "Consciousness Raising: A Radical Weapon," in *Feminist Revolution* (New York: Random House, 1978).

43. Freeman, *Politics of Women's Liberation*, 85, describes surging membership in NOW just after the first national women's rights demonstration. "Betty Friedan's Women's Strike on August 26, 1970," *New York Times*, March 23, 1970.

44. Sidney Tarrow, "Struggle, Politics, and Reform: Collective Action, Social Movements, and Cycles of Protest" (Cornell Western Societies Paper No. 21, Ithaca, N.Y.: Cornell University Press, 1989), 11.

45. Hernandez went on to help found the National Black Feminist Organization in 1973, and there is some suggestion that her quick departure involved charges of institutional racism.

4. Out of the Mainstream, into the Revolution?

1. Ronald Hrebenar, *Interest Group Politics in America*, 3d ed. (New York: M. E. Sharpe, 1997), 8.

2. Michael Goldfield, *The Decline of Organized Labor in the United States* (Chicago: University of Chicago Press, 1987), 238.

3. This view is shared by scholars such as Suzanne Staggenborg, *The Pro-Choice Movement: Organization and Activism in the Abortion Conflict* (New York: Oxford University Press, 1991), and William Gamson, *The Strategy of Social Protest* (Homewood, Ill.: Dorsey Press, 1975/1990).

4. Memo from Karen DeCrow to Politics Task Force, National Officers and Board Members, Chapter Presidents and Conveners, June 26, 1972. Involvement in the Republican convention seemed less intense. In the memo DeCrow noted that three NOW members planned to testify at the Republican platform hearings and requested that others inform her if they also planned to participate.

5. Toni Carabillo, Judith Meuli, and June Bundy Csida, *Feminist Chronicles* (Los Angeles: Women's Graphics, 1993), 50.

6. National Board Meeting Minutes, July 1975.

7. Memo from Jan Pittman-Liebman, Legislative Vice President, and Casey Hughes, Director of Legislative Office, to NOW National Board of Directors, July 23, 1975.

8. *DO IT NOW*, March/April 1975.

9. *DO IT NOW*, March/April 1975.

10. Minutes, National Board Meeting, April 1976.

11. *DO IT NOW*, January/February 1975.
12. *DO IT NOW*, January/February 1975.
13. Letter from Fran Kolb to Wilma Scott Heide, December 11, 1973.
14. Letter from Kolb to Heide, December 11, 1973.
15. Memo, Beverly Jones, Chair of Board Organization Committee, to National Board, January 1976.
16. Memo, Beverly Jones, to National Board, January 1976.
17. Memo, Beverly Jones, to National Board, January 1976.
18. "NOW, It's Money" (n.d.).
19. Memo from Midwest Regional Director Mary Anne Sedey to NOW Board, January 1976.
20. Eleanor Cutri Smeal, interview, July 2003.
21. "Pro Statement, Proposed NOW Bylaws," by Sandy Roth and Lillian Waugh, October 17, 1976.
22. Letter to Gene Kolb from Jo Ann Evans Gardner, December 11, 1973.
23. Lois Galgay Reckitt, "One Moment in Time," unpublished manuscript, n.d., 22.
24. See letter from Seattle Ad Hoc Committee to National Board, March 13, 1975.
25. "Call to Philadelphia Conference," May/June 1975.
26. Letter from Seattle Ad Hoc Committee to National Board, March 13, 1975.
27. Reckitt, "One Moment," 9–10.
28. "Call to Philadelphia Conference," May/June 1975.
29. Letter from Seattle Ad Hoc Committee to National Board, March 13, 1975.
30. Memo to National NOW officers and Board Members from Martha Buck and Mary Anne Sedey, March 22, 1976.
31. National Board Meeting Minutes, July 30–31, 1977.
32. Soon thereafter the League of Women Voters and the YWCA voted to lobby for the ERA. By 1973 the AFL-CIO also reversed its long-standing opposition to the amendment, and in this year eight more states voted for ratification.
33. Reckitt, "One Moment," 5.
34. Reckitt, "One Moment," 6.
35. Letter from Eastern Regional Director Jacqueline Ceballos to Jo Ann Evans Gardner, 1973.
36. Memo from Chris Guerrero to National Board Members, April 3, 1976.
37. On the dynamic among women's organizations, political parties, and the ERA, see Jo Freeman, "Political Culture of the Democratic and Republican Parties," *Political Science Quarterly* 3 (1986): 327–56; and Jo Freeman, "Who You Know vs. Who You Represent: Feminist Influence in the Democratic and Republican Parties," in *The Women's Movements of the United States and Western Europe: Feminist Consciousness, Political Opportunity, and Public Policy*, ed. Mary Fainsod Katzenstein and Carol McClurg Mueller (Philadelphia: Temple University Press, 1987); Christina Wolbrecht, *The Politics of Women's Rights: Parties, Positions, and Change* (Princeton: Princeton University Press, 2000); and Kira Sanbonmatsu, *Democrats, Republicans, and the Politics of Women's Place* (Ann Arbor: University of Michigan Press, 2002).
38. Memo from Charlene Suneson to Board of Directors, October 12, 1973.
39. Memo from Suneson to Board of Directors, October 12, 1973.
40. Memo from Suneson to Board of Directors, October 12, 1973.
41. Reckitt, "One Moment," 27.
42. See, for example, "Memo to NOW Board Members from Legislative Task Force, Florida State Legislative Coordinator," March 8, 1976. Jane Mansbridge, *Why*

We Lost the ERA (Chicago: University of Chicago Press, 1986), notes the tension that erupted between NOW and its partners in Illinois when the local NOW group insisted on staging a demonstration during a critical point in state legislative deliberation.

43. National NOW Conference Transcript, April 22–24, 1977, a.m. and p.m. sessions, 113–14.

44. National NOW Conference Transcript, 113–14.

45. National NOW Conference Transcript, 28–29.

46. National NOW Conference Transcript, 39–40.

47. Memo from Esther Kaw, Vice-President of Public Relations, to National NOW Board of Directors, April 3, 1976.

48. *DO IT NOW*, January/February 1975.

5. The ERA "Emergency"

1. On the ERA campaign, see Jane Mansbridge, *Why We Lost the ERA* (Chicago: University of Chicago Press, 1986).

2. Judy Mann, "NOW Decides to Stress ERA Ratification Drive," *Washington Post*, October 9, 1978.

3. National Board Meeting Minutes, February 1978.

4. National NOW Conference Transcript, 1978, 62.

5. "Total ERA Mobilization Voted," *National NOW Times*, October/November 1980.

6. Enid Nemy, "Commissions for Women's Conference Stress Economic Issues," *New York Times*, June 16, 1980.

7. "Summary of National Board Meetings, October 2, 1980," *National NOW Times*, October/November 1980.

8. "Summary of National Board Meeting: April 24–26, 1981," *National NOW Times*, September 1981.

9. Mansbridge, *Why We Lost the ERA*. For an interesting insight into the confusion even in Congress, see Robert Sherrill, "That Equal-Rights Amendment—What, Exactly, Does It Mean?" *New York Times*, September 20, 1970.

10. Mansbridge, *Why We Lost the ERA*.

11. Judy Mann, "NOW Comes of Age in the Political Arena: NOW Leaders Learn to Be Taken Seriously," *The Washington Post*, October 13, 1978.

12. David S. Broder, "New Liberal Alliance Warns Democrats," *Washington Post*, October 18, 1978; see also, for example, "Abzug Colleagues Resign to Protest Ouster by Carter," *Washington Post*, January 14, 1979.

13. Judy Mann, "Carter's New Advisers on Women Seem Safe," *Washington Post*, May 11, 1979.

14. Marshall Ingewerson, "The Advocacy Race: Political Right, Left Vie for Money, Members, Power," *Christian Science Monitor*, December 29, 1980.

15. "Right-Wing Victory Claims Distorted," *National NOW Times*, December/January 1980–81.

16. Letter from Eleanor Smeal, National NOW Conference Book, 1980.

17. Roberta Spalter-Roth and Ronnee Schreiber, "Outsider Issues and Insider Tactics: Strategic Tensions in the Women's Policy Network during the 1980s," in *Feminist Organizations: Harvest of the New Women's Movement*, ed. Myra Marx Ferree and Patricia Yancey Martin (Philadelphia: Temple University Press, 1995), 105.

18. "1980 Conference Resolutions, 1980 Presidential Elections," *National NOW Times*, October/November 1980.

19. "1980 Conference Resolutions."

20. Spalter-Roth and Schreiber, "Outsider Issues," 112. See also Patricia Ireland, *What Women Want* (New York: Penguin Books, 1996), 167–70.

21. On the social movement politics of this issue, see Suzanne Staggenborg, *The Pro-Choice Movement: Organization and Activism in the Abortion Conflict* (New York: Oxford University Press, 1991) and Karen O'Connor, *No Neutral Ground? Abortion Politics in an Age of Absolutes* (Boulder, Colo.: Westview Press, 1996).

22. Lynn Darling, "Abortion Funding a Hot Issue in Area Courts and Clinics," *Washington Post*, November 29, 1977.

23. Megan Rosenfeld, "Waging the War of the Roses: The Banners of 'Pro-Life' and 'Pro-Choice' Meet on the Capitol Hill Battlefield," *Washington Post*, January 23, 1979; Bernard Weinraub, "Liberal Groups Report Surge since Reagan Election," *New York Times*, December 9, 1980.

24. Ireland, *What Women Want*, 167–68.

25. Jane Wells-Schooley, "Reagan Leads Republican Assault on Abortion, Birth Control," *National NOW Times*, August 1982.

26. See, for example, Ellen Goodman, "At Large," *National NOW Times*, November 1981. Toni Carabillo, Judith Meuli, and June Bundy Csida, *Feminist Chronicles* (Los Angeles: Women's Graphics, 1993), 108.

27. In 1988, for example, the Women's Campaign Fund (WCF) provided the spark for the inclusion of a new plank in both parties' platforms that encouraged the recruitment of and support for women candidates.

28. Center for American Women in Politics, *News and Notes*, July 1983.

29. Myra Marx Ferree and Beth B. Hess, *Controversy and Coalition: The New Feminist Movement* (Boston: Twayne, 1985), 118.

30. Flora Davis, *Moving the Mountain: The Women's Movement in America since 1960* (Urbana: University of Illinois Press, 1999), 415–32. "Women Vote Differently than Men: Feminist Bloc Emerges in 1980 Elections," *National NOW Times*, December/January 1980–81.

31. "Women Seen as Major Political Force," *National NOW Times*, April 1982.

32. On the mixed messages embedded in these surveys, see Mansbridge, *Why We Lost the ERA*.

33. Carabillo, Meuli, and Csida, *Feminist Chronicles*, 91.

34. Adam Clymer, "Board of NOW to Oppose Carter, Charging Lag on Women's Issues," *New York Times*, December 11, 1979. One board member said that the board "left the NOW political action arm free 'to do what's politically expedient' later." Barry Sussman, "Gallup Poll Cites Big Turnaround in Carter's Strength," *Washington Post*, December 12, 1979.

35. Leslie Bennetts, "NOW's Carter Stand Perplexes Feminists," *New York Times*, December 12, 1979.

36. Alice Bonner, "New Success for Women: More Seek Elective Office," *Washington Post*, October 18, 1978.

37. "Democratic Rules Committee to Offer Strong 'Equal Division' Proposals," *National NOW Times*, August 1980.

38. "Feminists Display Clout at Democratic Convention," *National NOW Times*, September 1980.

39. Megan Rosenfeld, "Women Join Forces in the Name of Politics," *Washington Post*, July 15, 1979.

40. Leslie Bennetts, "Women in Office: How Have They Affected Women's Issues?" *Washington Post*, November 4, 1980.

41. "1980 Conference Resolutions."

42. "The Significance of the Democratic Convention," *National NOW Times*, September 1980, 7.

43. "Feminists Display Clout."

44. "Feminists Display Clout."

45. Mansbridge, *Why We Lost the ERA*.

46. Bill Peterson, "ERA Backers Take Different Tack in North Carolina," *Washington Post*, February 12, 1979; Ferree and Hess, *Controversy and Coalition*, 113–14.

47. "1981 Conference Resolutions, Political Action for Reproductive Rights," *National NOW Times*, October 1981.

48. *New York Times*, January 6, 1979.

49. Megan Rosenfeld, "Va. Group Seeks ERA Approval; Women in Va. Press for ERA Backing," *Washington Post*, January 14, 1978. Soon thereafter several states' attorneys general, including Missouri's John Ashcroft, filed antitrust suits against NOW to block it from pursuing this activity.

50. "Thousands Expected to Join in 'Rescue the ERA' March," *Washington Post*, July 8, 1978.

51. "1981 Conference Resolutions, ERA," *National NOW Times*, October 1981.

52. Joanne Omang, "Smeal: Organized, Tough, with Steely Determination," *Washington Post*, October 9, 1979.

53. Joanne Omang, "Feuding Women's Groups Agree on Issues," *Washington Post*, October 20, 1979.

54. Joanne Omang, "NOW Launching Political Push on Issues," *Washington Post*, October 9, 1979.

55. Omang, "NOW Launching Political Push."

56. Joanne Omang, "NOW Votes to Intensify Boycott in Support of ERA," *Washington Post*, October 8, 1979.

57. "24 Groups Urge HEW Hearings on Abortion Funding Restraints," *Washington Post*, January 21, 1978; Spencer Rich, "Coalition Aims to Block Cuts in Social Security," *Washington Post*, January 19, 1979.

58. Judy Klemesrud, "Complacency on Abortion: A Warning to Women," *New York Times*, January 23, 1978.

59. William H. Jones, "Four Groups Try to Block WJLA Sale," *Washington Post*, February 3, 1978; Ernest Holsendolph, "Rights Organizations Plan to Monitor Hiring by Broadcast Stations," *New York Times*, July 2, 1980.

60. "Bill on Prostitution," *Washington Post*, February 25, 1978.

61. Cynthia Corney, "The Insurance Industry Comes under Fire on Two Fronts; Antitrust Actions against 25 Firms Filed in California," *Washington Post*, August 29, 1978, D9.

62. Leslie Bennetts, "For the Problems Women Have in Common, Finding Sources of Help," *New York Times*, December 23, 1978.

63. Karen Dewitt, "Women Briefed on Arms Talks," *New York Times*, December 8, 1978.

64. The coded data used in this analysis have at least three notable limitations. First, although the data give indications about the types of strategies and actions discussed and agreed on in national board meetings, the number of approved resolutions in board meetings does not necessarily reflect the number of resources and amount of time spent by the organization implementing or pursuing this strategy. NOW is a large, chapter-based organization, and much of its activity takes place on the local level. Chapters are linked to national NOW for financing, for the publications NOW produces, and for the action initiatives planned by the NOW leadership but also enjoy a great deal of autonomy in choosing the activities in which they will participate. Never-

theless, the data give a picture of the types of issues on which the NOW Board reached consensus and how these issues changed, if at all, over time. Second, a significant amount of time during board meetings was spent debating motions and issues that ultimately failed; but this analysis focuses only on consensus initiatives. Finally, an analysis of the distribution of resolutions passed by the NOW Board suggests only what the board was doing, not why it was doing it. Although the board minutes suggest changes of strategic emphasis over time, an understanding of why they occurred and their importance to the organization requires an analysis of supplementary materials.

For every national board meeting between 1969 and 1983 for which minutes were available, I analyzed eight categories of motions, representing 80 percent of all motions approved (Table 5.1). (Board meeting minutes were unavailable for June, October, and December 1976; April and July 1982; and December 1983.) I coded every motion that passed during a board meeting according to the strategy or action to which it referred. (Thus three motions in one board meeting might refer to a protest/grassroots strategy. If all these motions passed, they were all included in the analysis even if they referred to the same action or built on a previous motion.)

65. "Total ERA Mobilization Voted," *National NOW Times*, October/November 1980.

66. "Congressional Sponsors Take New Initiative in Campaign," *National NOW Times*, April 1982.

67. Leslie Bennetts, "Equal Rights Plan's Backers Vow to Defeat Opposition Legislators," *New York Times*, June 20, 1980.

68. See Mansbridge's detailed examination of this support in *Why We Lost the ERA.*

69. Louis Harris, "ERA Support Soars as Deadline Nears," *National NOW Times*, June/July 1982.

70. "ERA Countdown Ends: Spurs Renewed Fight for Equality," *National NOW Times*, August 1982.

71. "ERA Countdown Ends."

72. "ERA Countdown Ends."

73. "Women Seen as Major Political Force."

74. See, for example, Leslie Bennetts, "Feminist Drive Is Likely to Persist Even If Rights Amendment Fails," *New York Times*, May 31, 1978; Judy Mann, "Women Understanding Power Structure Better," *Washington Post*, May 2, 1979.

75. "NOW Seeking $3 Million War Chest to Oust ERA Foes, Fight New Right," *National NOW Times*, September 1982.

76. "Unprecedented Numbers of Women File in Florida State Races Post-ERA," *National NOW Times*, August 1982, 1.

77. Ireland, *What Women Want*, 135–36.

78. "A President with a Pragmatic Approach," *National NOW Times*, October 1982.

79. Omang, "NOW Launching Political Push."

80. "Republicans Block Equality for Women," *National NOW Times*, March 1982. The bipartisan NWPC felt similarly disenchanted—if not disgusted—with the Republicans and especially Reagan. Davis, *Moving the Mountain*, 424.

6. From the ERA Strategy to the Electoral Strategy

1. Felicity Barringer, "NOW Reasserts Its Role as Outsider," *New York Times*, January 12, 1992.

2. Spalter-Roth and Schreiber, "Outsider Issues," 115.

3. Spalter-Roth and Schreiber, "Outsider Issues," 115.

4. Jo Freeman, "Who You Know vs. Who You Represent: Feminist Influence in the Democratic and Republican Parties," in *The Women's Movements of the United States and Western Europe: Feminist Consciousness, Political Opportunity, and Public Policy*, ed. Mary Katzenstein and Carol McClurg Mueller (Philadelphia: Temple University Press, 1987), 241.

5. "ERA Countdown Ends: Spurs Renewed Fight for Equality," *National NOW Times*, August 1982.

6. "Summary of National Board Meeting, December 4–5, 1982," *National NOW Times*, November/December 1982, 11.

7. "Campaign Notes: Registering of 250,000 Is Reported by NOW," *New York Times*, October 20, 1984.

8. "ERA Countdown Ends."

9. "Yes, Ronnie, There Really Is a Gender Gap!" *National NOW Times*, November/December 1982.

10. "ERA Countdown Ends."

11. Patricia Ireland, *What Women Want* (New York: Penguin Books, 1996), 135.

12. Ireland, *What Women Want*, 263.

13. "ERA Supporters Win Major Victories in NC Primaries," *National NOW Times*, August 1982.

14. "NOW PACs Seek $3 Million to Fight Right Wing Assault" *National NOW Times*, September 1982.

15. John Herbers, "Women Turn View to Public Office," *New York Times*, June 29, 1982; "NOW PACs Seek $3 Million."

16. National NOW Conference Book, 1983.

17. "PAC/Woman Walk to Raise Funds for Feminist Candidates," *National NOW Times*, August 1982.

18. Four types of PACs are affiliated with NOW: NOW/EQUALITY/PAC, a national NOW PAC for state and local races; NOW/PAC, the PAC for federal races; and the NOW chapter and state PACs.

19. See Jeffrey M. Berry, *The Interest Group Society*, 3d ed. (New York: Longman, 1997), 17–43.

20. Sandra Salmans, "The Rising Force of Women's PAC's," *New York Times*, June 28, 1984.

21. Barbara Basler, "Democrats Discuss Woman on Ticket," *New York Times*, March 13, 1984.

22. Perlez, "Women, Power, and Politics"; Toni Carabillo, Judith Meuli, and June Bundy Csida, *Feminist Chronicles* (Los Angeles: Women's Graphics, 1993), 109.

23. Iver Peterson, "G.O.P. Starts Training in 'Gender Gap' Politics," *New York Times*, June 6, 1983.

24. "NOW Vows New Campaign to Win ERA," *National NOW Times*, March 1983.

25. "Rights Amendment Stressed as Major 1984 Election Issue," *New York Times*, November 13, 1983.

26. Perlez, "Women, Power, and Politics."

27. Flora Davis, *Moving the Mountain*: The Women's Movement in America since 1960 (Urbana: University of Illinois Press, 1999), 420.

28. Perlez, "Women, Power, and Politics."

29. Fay S. Joyce, "6 Democrats Appeal for Backing at NOW Parley," *New York Times*, October 3, 1983.

30. Bernard Weinraub, "Women's Endorsement Seems a 2-way Race," *New York Times*, December 2, 1983.

31. "Endorsement Set by Women's Group," *New York Times*, October 1, 1983.

32. Bernard Weinraub, "NOW, in First Endorsement, Backs Mondale," *New York Times*, December 11, 1983.

33. Barbara Basler, "Mondale Effort in Florida Hinges on Little and Big NOW Chapters," *New York Times*, March 6, 1984.

34. Basler, "Mondale Effort."

35. Perlez, "Women, Power, and Politics."

36. Sandra Salmans, "Mondale Warned by Women's Group," *New York Times*, June 30, 1984.

37. Sandra Salmans, "NOW Resolution Meeting Opposition of Feminists," *New York Times*, July 4, 1984.

38. Bernard Weinraub, "23 Prominent Women to Support Mondale Even if He Picks a Man," *New York Times*, July 5, 1984.

39. Maureen Dowd, "Caucuses are S.R.O. and Joy Surprises Women at Convention," *New York Times*, July 20, 1984.

40. Sandra Salmans, "How Much Feminists Influenced Choice of Ferraro Is Debated," *New York Times*, July 28, 1984.

41. "Party Urged to Pick Women," *New York Times*, May 10, 1988.

42. Richard L. Berke, "Women Accusing Democrats of Betrayal," *New York Times*, October 17, 1991.

43. Carabillo, Meuli, and Csida, *Feminist Chronicles*, 133.

44. Barringer, "NOW Reasserts Its Role."

45. Peter Applebome, "Religious Right Intensifies Campaign for Bush," *New York Times*, October 31, 1992.

46. Richard L. Berke, "Women Discover the Political Power of Raising Money for Their Own," *New York Times*, May 31, 1992.

47. Amy Handlin, *Whatever Happened to the Year of the Woman? Why Women are Still Not Making It to the Top in Politics* (Denver: Arden Press, 1998); Majorie R. Hershey, "The Congressional Elections," in *The Election of 1992*, ed. Gerald M. Pomper (Chatham, N.J.: Chatham House, 1993); Kim Fridkin Kahn and Edie N. Goldenberg, "The Media: Ally or Obstacle of Feminists?" *The Annals of the American Academy of Political and Social Science*, 515 (1991): 104-13.

48. Carabillo, Meuli, and Csida, *Feminist Chronicles*, 147.

49. David Shribman, "Interest Groups Are Going Corporate for Advice," *New York Times*, October 16, 1993.

50. Barringer, "NOW Reasserts Its Role."

51. "Goldsmith Speech to 1982 NOW Conference," *National NOW Times*, October 1982.

52. "NOW Vows New Campaign."

53. "Summary of National Board Meeting, December 4–5, 1982."

54. "1982 Conference Resolutions, Feminist Consciousness Raising Resolution," *National NOW Times*, October 1982.

55. "Goldsmith Speech to 1982 NOW Conference," *National NOW Times*, October 1982.

56. Spalter-Roth and Schreiber, "Outsider Issues," 122.

57. Robin Toner, "Democrats and Women: Party Shifts Approach," *New York Times*, July 11, 1987.

58. Enid Nemy, "Feminist Cause Looks Back to Grass Roots," *New York Times*, November 8, 1982.

59. Phil Gialey, "NOW Chief Describes Plans to Fight 'Fascists and Bigots,'" *New York Times*, September 6, 1985.

60. "Women Weren't Born Democrat, Republican, or Yesterday," *National NOW Times*, October 1982.

61. Salmans, "Rising Force of Women's PAC's."

62. "NOW Supporting Some Men Instead of Women for Office," *New York Times*, October 3, 1982. Conflicts regularly arose within chapters over endorsements as well. In 1990 the California NOW chapter, for example, had a difficult debate over supporting Dianne Feinstein for the Democratic nomination for governor over Attorney General John K. Van de Kamp, a strong feminist supporter. In the end, the chapter withheld its support for either candidate in the primary. Robert Reinhold, "California Race Is Becoming Symbolic for Women," *New York Times*, June 4, 1990.

63. Weinraub, "NOW, in First Endorsement, Backs Mondale."

64. Barbara Balster, "G.O.P. Starting Campaign to Show 'Reagan Is Terrific' on Women's Issues," *New York Times*, April 6, 1984.

65. Eleanor Cutri Smeal, interview, July 2003.

66. John Herbers, "Women Turn View to Public Office," *New York Times*, June 28, 1982.

67. E. J. Dionne Jr., "Women's Caucus Is Focusing on Abortion Rights," *New York Times*, August 6, 1989.

68. "NOW: Patricia Ireland, President of NOW," *New York Times*, March 1, 1992.

69. Interview with Eleanor Cutri Smeal, July 2003.

70. "NOW Urges a New Party," *New York Times*, September 16, 1991.

71. Jane Gross, "At NOW Convention, Goal Is Putting More Women in Office," *New York Times*, July 1, 1990.

72. Carabillo, Meuli, and Csida, *Feminist Chronicles*, 148.

73. Interview with Patricia Ireland, August 4, 2003.

74. Nadine Brozan, "A President with a Pragmatic Approach," *New York Times*, October 11, 1982.

75. "Goldsmith Speech to 1982 NOW Conference"; Brozan, "President with a Pragmatic Approach."

76. Davis, *Moving the Mountain*, 421.

77. Perlez, "Women, Power, and Politics."

78. Gross, "NOW: Patricia Ireland."

79. Davis, *Moving the Mountain*, 415–34.

80. Maureen Dowd, "Political Outlook Dims for Women after Hopes Raised by Ferraro's Bid," *New York Times*, November 1, 1984.

81. Robin Toner, "NOW Marks 20th Year amid a Strategy Debate," *New York Times*, June 13, 1986.

82. Interview with NOW Vice President Executive Kim Gandy, April 12, 2000.

83. Nadine Brozan, "Smeal and Goldsmith Fight for Leadership of NOW," *New York Times*, June 8, 1985.

84. Judy Klemesrud, "Crucial Election Looms at Feminist Convention," *New York Times*, July 19, 1985.

85. Brozan, "Smeal and Goldsmith."

86. Brozan, "Smeal and Goldsmith."

87. Klemesrud, "NOW's President."

88. Judy Klemesrud, "New Head of NOW Prefers Activism," *New York Times*, July 22, 1985.

89. Phil Gialey, "NOW Chief Describes Plans to Fight 'Fascists and Bigots,' " *New York Times*, September 6, 1985.

90. Gialey, "NOW Chief Describes Plans."

91. Toner, "NOW Marks 20th Year."

92. Toner, "NOW Marks 20th Year."

93. Greenhouse, "After Bork."

94. Linda Greenhouse, "Opponents Find Judge Souter Is a Hard Choice to Oppose," *New York Times*, September 9, 1990.

95. Evelyn Nieves, "With Rising Voice, Acting Head of Feminist Group Assumes Mantle," *New York Times*, July 7, 1991.

96. Suro, "Thomas Foes."

97. The *Akron* decision found statutes that mandated that first-trimester abortions must be performed in hospitals to be unconstitutional. *Thornburgh* struck down statutes that required doctors to tell women about the risks of abortion procedures and assistance available from the state for pregnant women.

98. "NOW Members Are Told to Seek New Allies in Fight on Abortion," *New York Times*, July 23, 1989.

99. Gross, "At NOW Convention."

100. Felicity Barringer, "Many Are Arrested at Abortion Clinic," *New York Times*, November 12, 1989.

101. Barringer, "Many Are Arrested," 33.

102. Barringer, "Many Are Arrested," 33.

103. Carabillo, Meuli, and Csida, *Feminist Chronicles*, 140.

104. NARAL, http://www.naral.org/mediaresources/fact/decisions.html.

105. Carabillo, Meuli, and Csida, "*Feminist Chronicles*, 146.

106. Robin Toner, "Rally against Abortion Hears Pledge of Support by Reagan," *New York Times*, January 23, 1987.

107. Carabillo, Meuli, and Csida, *Feminist Chronicles*, 141.

108. Felicity Barringer, "Planned Parenthood: Quiet Cause to Focus of Fury," *New York Times*, October 30, 1990.

109. E. J. Dionne Jr., "Many Legislatures Will Try to Follow Example Set by Missouri Law," *New York Times*, July 4, 1989.

110. Felicity Barringer, "They Keep the Abortion Protest Alive," *New York Times*, January 23, 1991.

111. Barringer, "They Keep the Abortion Protest Alive."

112. Dudley Celdinen, "U.S. Sends Warning of Potential Threat to Abortion Clinics," *New York Times*, January 11, 1985.

113. John Herbers, "NOW Seeks to Curb Anti-Abortionists," *New York Times*, January 11, 1986; Nadine Brozan, "503 Held in Abortion Protest on East 85th Street," *New York Times*, May 3, 1988.

114. Gerald M. Boyd, "Reagan Condemns Arson at Clinics," *New York Times*, January 4, 1985.

115. Jonathan Fuerbringer, "80,000 in March to Capitol to Back Right to Abortion," *New York Times*, March 10, 1986.

116. NOW Foundation Annual Report 1997, http://www.nowfoundation.org/annual/97report.html; Herbers, "NOW Seeks to Curb Anti-Abortionists"; Tamar Lewin, "Abortion Foes Lose Appeal over Rackets Law Damages," *New York Times*, March 4, 1989.

117. "NOW Leader Sees Big Turnout at Abortion Rights March," *New York*

Times, April 8, 1989; "NOW Goes to Court to Deter Blocking of Abortion Clinics," *New York Times*, April 28, 1989.

118. Catherine S. Manegold, "Abortion War, Buffalo Front: Top Guns Use Battle Tactics," *New York Times*, April 25, 1992.

119. Carabillo, Meuli, and Csida, *Feminist Chronicles*, 147.

120. "Anti-Abortion Group to Close Headquarters," *New York Times*, February 1, 1990.

121. Manegold, "Abortion War, Buffalo Front."

122. E. J. Dionne, "Struggle for Work and Family Fueling Women's Movement," *New York Times*, August 22, 1989.

123. Toner, "NOW Marks 20th Year"; Dionne, "Women's Caucus."

124. Carabillo, Meuli, and Csida, *Feminist Chronicles*, 146.

125. E. J. Dionne Jr., "Tepid Black Support Worries Advocates of Abortion Rights," *New York Times*, April 16, 1989; Catherine S. Manegold, "Beyond Topic A: The Battle over Choice Obscures Other Vital Concerns of Women," *New York Times*, August 2, 1992.

126. Manegold, "Beyond Topic A"; Marianne Szegedy-Maszak, "Calm, Cool, and Beleaguered," *New York Times*, August 6, 1989; Dionne, "Women's Caucus."

127. David Margolick, "Seeking Strength in Independence, Abortion-Rights Unit Quits A.C.L.U.," *New York Times*, May 21, 1992.

128. "Left and Right Fight for Custody of 'Family' Issue," *New York Times*, August 20, 1987.

129. Quoted in Gross, "NOW: Patricia Ireland," 18.

130. Dionne, "Struggle for Work and Family"; Dionne, "Women's Caucus."

131. Gross, "NOW: Patricia Ireland," 18.

7. The Clinton Years and Beyond

1. Art Levine and Amy Cunningham, "Post-Triumph Trauma: For the Long-Suffering Left, Winning Can Feel Weird," *Washington Post*, November 29, 1992. See also Harriet Woods's recent memoir, *Up to Power: The Political Journey of American Women* (Boulder: Westview Press, 2000).

2. Levine and Cunningham, "Post-Triumph Trauma." When the group formed in 1969, early in the abortion rights movement, it called itself the "National Association for the Repeal of Abortion Laws," but in 1973 NARAL adopted a new name, "the National Abortion Rights Action League."

3. Ruth Marcus, "Clinton Berates Critics in Women's Groups," *Washington Post*, December 22, 1992.

4. Vanessa Gallman, "President Signs New Welfare Deal but Ally Calls It 'Moment of Shame,'" *Detroit Free Press*, August 23, 1996.

5. Patricia Ireland, "Clinton, Our Option, Not Our Answer," *National NOW Times*, November 1996.

6. "NOW Statements and Articles on Jones v. Clinton," http://www.now.org/issues/harass/jones.html; "NOW Statements and Articles on Allegations against President Clinton," http://www.now.org/issues/harass/clinton.html. "Statement of NOW President Patricia Ireland Calling for Fair Treatment of Jones' Suit, Questioning Right Wing's Disingenuous Fervor," May 6, 1994, http://www.now.org/issues/harass/jones.html.

7. See, for example, commentary on Rightgrrl's Web page, "NOW Watch"; many documents at NOW's Web site, http://www.now.org, including press releases "NOW Calls on Clinton to Forswear 'Nuts or Sluts' Defense, Work with Congress to

Strengthen Women's Rights Laws," and "NOW President Patricia Ireland Challenges Livingston to Rein in Conservatives and Calls upon Women to Lobby against Impeachment," December 11, 1998. See also press releases from the Independent Women's Forum, including "Women's Group Demands That Paula Jones Have Her 'Day in Court'"; "Notes Hypocrisy of NOW, Other Women's Groups"; and news reporting from Justin Blum, "Dissenting Dulles Chapter Wages High-Profile Battle within NOW," *Washington Post*, June 1, 1998; Terry M. Neal and Thomas B. Edsall, "Allegations against Clinton Leave Women's Groups Conflicted about Responding," *Washington Post*, January 30, 1988.

8. "Letter from Patricia Ireland to the Media about Portrayal of NOW," April 1998, http://www.now.org/press/04–98/letter-ed.html.

9. Patricia Ireland, interview, August 4, 2003.

10. Blum, "Dissenting Dulles Chapter."

11. Toni Carabillo, Judith Meuli, and June Bundy Csida, *Feminist Chronicles* (Los Angeles: Women's Graphics, 1993), 143.

12. Statement by an anonymous NOW official in a workshop at NOW's national conference in Miami, 2000.

13. I obtained this figure by tallying the number of chapters one may join from NOW's Web site (identified as codes for individuals to enter into their membership application), http://www.now.org.

14. "Prizes Added to Mega-Membership Drive: Extra Incentives Boost Participation," *National NOW Times*, May 1997, http://www.now.org/nnt/05–97/megamemb .html.

15. Information from fiscal year 1997 data drawn from financial information collected by Philanthropic Research, Inc., http://www.guidestar.com.

16. Carabillo, Meuli, and Csida, *Feminist Chronicles*, 138.

17. Both drives were "essentially failures," according to Lois Galgay Reckitt (written comment to author, 2000).

18. Carabillo, Meuli, and Csida, *Feminist Chronicles*, 120.

19. Of more than three thousand documents available at NOW's Web site, this is the only one that refers to NOW's income and expenses. "1997 Budget," http://www.now.org/nnt/05–97/budget.html.

20. "Mega-Membership Drive Amplifies NOW's Voice; Payoff Includes Prizes— and New Members," *National NOW Times*, March 1997, http://www.now.org.nnt .03–97/mega.html.

21. "Membership Contest Increases Activist Ranks," *National NOW Times*, October 1997, http://www.now.org/nnt/10–97/memb.html.

22. "Connecting Grassroots Activists and NOW Action Center a Priority," *National NOW Times*, Winter 1999, http://www.now.org/nnt/winter-99/activists.html.

23. "Technological Equipment and Service Needs," http://www.now.org/orga niza/computer.html.

24. "About the NOW Foundation," http://www.nowfoundation.org/about.html.

25. The National Organization for Women Foundation Annual Report, 1994, http://www.nowfoundation.org/board94.html.

26. These observations derive from notes I took of discussions at NOW's 2000 national conference in Miami, at the Young Feminist Caucus and at the "Other Issues" hearing.

27. "Spark! Voices and Views of NOW Feminists," Florida Young Feminist Task Force, June 2000.

28. Catherine S. Manegold, "No More Nice Girls: In Angry Droves, Radical Feminists Just Want to Have Impact," *New York Times*, July 12, 1992.

29. Manegold, "No More Nice Girls."

30. Rebecca Walker, "Revisioning the Battlefield: New Leadership in Difficult Times," speech delivered at the National NOW Conference, Arlington, Va., July 17, 2003.

31. NOW Bylaws, 2003, http://www.now.org/organization/bylaws.html?printable.

32. NOW Foundation Annual Report, 1997, http://www.nowfoundation.org/annual/97report.html.

33. This action can be seen as self-serving, however, as affirmative action is a major benefit for white women.

34. National NOW Conference Resolutions, "Recognition of NOW's Commitment to Economic Justice," 2001, http://www.now.org/organization/conference/resolutions/2001.htm.

35. "Statement by Board Members of the National Organization for Women," May 1996, http://now.org.nnt/05-96/tambwoc.html.

36. 1999 National NOW Conference Resolutions, http://www.now.org/nnt/fall-99/resolutions.html.

37. NOW Bylaws, Article IV, Section 5, http://www.now.org/organization/bylaws.html#VIISection6.

38. National NOW Conference Resolutions, "Rededicating Ourselves to Eliminating Racism," 2001, http://www.now.org/organization/conference/resolutions/2001.html.

39. Suzanne Rumph, "Black and White NOW Members Talk about the Racial Diversification of the National Organization for Women," Master's thesis, Wayne State University, 2000.

40. "NOW Names New Director of Racial Diversity Programs," January 8, 2004, http://www.now.org/press/01-04/01-08a.html.

41. "1995 National NOW Conference Resolutions," http://www.now.org/organization/conference/1995/resoluti.html. This change would have the effect of raising the category of sex to the level of strict scrutiny applied to that of race in cases before the U.S. Supreme Court.

42. Jane Gross, "NOW: Patricia Ireland, President of NOW" *New York Times*, March 1, 1992; Megan Rosenfeld, "The NOW and Future Feminist: New President Patricia Ireland Taking a '90s Tack on Persistent Problems," *Washington Post*, January 11, 1992.

43. Jan Welch, interview, July 2003.

44. Interviews with author, June 2000.

45. Lois Galgay Reckitt, interview and written comments to author, 2000.

46. See Christina Wolbrecht, *The Politics of Women's Rights: Parties, Positions, and Change* (Princeton: Princeton University Press, 2000); Kira Sanbonmatsu, *Democrats, Republicans, and the Politics of Women's Place* (Ann Arbor: University of Michigan Press, 2002).

47. Interview with author, March 23, 1993.

48. EMILY's List, http://emilyslist.com/el-newsstand/pr/1999/990729–nrcc.asp.

49. Thomas B. Edsall, "Show of Party Unity Masks Scars of Ideological Battle: Center Wins Day in Democrats' Tug of War," *Washington Post*, July 13, 1992.

50. "Testimony on the 1996 Democratic National Platform to the Platform Committee," August 5, 1996, http://now.org/issues/elections/platforms96.html; 1996 Democratic Party Platform, http://www.democrats.org/hq/resources/platform/platform.html.

51. http://www.now.org/nnt/11–96/elex.html.

52. http://www.now.org/nnt/winter-99/electns.html.

53. http://www.now.org/nnt/winter-99/electns.html.

54. http://www.now.org/nnt/fall-98/elect.html.

55. http://www.now.org/nnt/fall-98/elect.html.

56. http://www.now.org/nnt/fall-98/elect.html; http://www.nowpacs.org/facts/html.

57. This technique allows EMILY's List to distribute huge sums; for example, in the 1997–98 election cycle, its members contributed $7.5 million to pro-choice Democratic women candidates. Though EMILY's List has few ideological requirements, it does demand that candidates prove their "viability." EMILY's List, http://emilyslist.com/el-newsstand/pr/1999/990729–nrcc.asp.

58. Open Secrets, http://www.opensecrets.org/pubs/bigpicture2000/industry/ideology.html.

59. According to data compiled by the Center for Responsive Politics, these races were in Wisconsin's District 2, Georgia's District 4, and Missouri's District 9.

60. Open Secrets, http://www.opensecrets.org/pacs/pacgot.asp?strid=C00092247&cycle=1998.

61. Open Secrets, http://www.opensecrets.org/pacs/industry.asp?txt=Q08&cycle=2000. In both the 1998 and 2000 election cycles NOW attracted fewer large (over $200) contributions than any other top women's issue PAC. http://www.opensecrets.org.

62. NOW, http://www.now.org/nnt/11–96/elex.html.

63. http://www.now.org/nnt/fall-99/pac.html.

64. 2002 National NOW Conference Resolutions, "2002 Elections," http://www.now.org/organization/conference/resolutions/2002/html.

65. "The Drive for Equality," http://www.now.org/organization/driveforequality/index.html.

66. See Susan Moller Okin, *Justice, Gender, and the Family* (New York: Basic Books, 1989); Sonya Michel and Rianne Mahon, eds., *Child Care Policy at the Crossroads: Gender and Welfare State Restructuring* (New York: Routledge, 2002); Suzanne W. Helburn and Barbara R. Bergmann, *America's Childcare Problem: The Way Out* (New York: Palgrave, 2002).

67. Mary Frances Berry, *The Politics of Parenthood: Child Care, Women's Rights, and the Myth of the Good Mother* (New York: Viking, 1993); Barbara Ehrenreich, "Doing It for Ourselves: Can Feminism Survive Class Polarization?" *In These Times*, November 29, 1999, http:// http://faculty.uml.edu/sgallagher/femclass.htm; Harriet Woods, *Stepping Up to Power: The Political Journey of American Women* (Boulder: Westview Press, 2000); Friedan, *Life So Far*; Ann Crittendon, *The Price of Motherhood: Why the Most Important Job in the World is Still the Least Valued* (New York: Metropolitan Books, 2001); Myra H. Strober, "Women in the Workplace—The Unfinished Revolution," *USA Today* (magazine), November 2003.

68. The 1999 National NOW Conference Resolutions, http://www.now.org/nnt/fall-99/resolutions.html; 2003 Workshops, http://www.now.org/organizations/conference/2003/workshops-old.html; "NOW Opposes the Rescinding of 'Baby UI,' Calls for Comprehensive Paid Family Leave, http://www.now.org/issues/family/013003ui-comments.html.

69. Gross, "NOW: Patricia Ireland," 54.

70. See Jocelyn Crowley, *The Politics of Child Support in America* (Cambridge: Cambridge University Press, 2003).

71. Crittenden, *The Price of Motherhood.*

72. See Theda Skocpol, *Social Policy in the United States: Future Possibilities in Historical Perspective* (Princeton: Princeton University Press, 1995).

73. "The Drive for Equality," http://www.now.org/organization/driveforequality/index.html.

74. "The Drive for Equality," http://www.now.org/organization/driveforequality/index.html.

75. Patricia Ireland, interview August 4, 2003.

76. Eleanor Cutri Smeal, interview, July 2003.

8. Analyzing Grassroots Representation and Participation

1. See Maryann Barakso, "Member Influence in Large Voluntary Associations," presented at the Annual Meeting of the Southern Political Science Association, Savannah, Georgia, November 6–9, 2002.

2. David S. Broder and Kenneth J. Cooper, "Revolt Brewing for NOW Election," *Washington Post*, June 20, 1993. Approximately three thousand delegates are allocated among the nine regions. Generally, between four hundred and twelve hundred delegates vote at national conferences.

3. Thomas B. Edsall, "Show of Party Unity Masks Scars of Ideological Battle: Center Wins Day in Democrats' Tug of War," *Washington Post*, July 13, 1992. In 2001 the president's salary was approximately $140,000. See also the statements of opposing slates in the *National NOW Times*, "Teams Come Forward for 1993 Election," June 1993.

4. Author's notes.

5. Harry C. Boyte, "On Silences and Civic Muscle, or Why Social Capital Is a Useful but Insufficient Concept," paper presented at the Havens Center, University of Wisconsin-Madison, April 10, 2001, 6.

6. Louis J. Ayala, "Trained for Democracy: The Differing Effects of Voluntary and Involuntary Organizations on Political Participation," *Political Research Quarterly* 53 (2002): 101. Although Ayala refers here to "nonpolitical organizations" such as the religious institutions described in Sidney Verba, Kay Lehman Schlozman, and Henry E. Brady, *Voice and Equality: Civic Voluntarism in American Politics* (Cambridge, Mass.: Belknap Press, 1995), there is no theoretical reason to assume that this statement does not apply to the skills transmitted through politically oriented voluntary associations. For more on the transference of civic skills and civic education through organizations, see Charles Payne, *I've Got the Light of Freedom: The Organizing Tradition of the Mississippi Freedom Struggle* (Berkeley: University of California Press, 1995); Roberta S. Sigel, *Political Learning in Adulthood* (Chicago: University of Chicago Press, 1989); and Robert Putnam, "Presidential Address to American Political Science Association," Boston, Mass., August 29, 2002.

7. Verba, Schlozman, and Brady, *Voice and Equality*, 353.

8. Pamela Paxton, "Social Capital and Democracy: An Interdependent Relationship," *American Sociological Review* 67 (2002): 255.

9. Sara Evans and Harry C. Boyte, *Free Spaces: The Source of Democratic Change in America* (New York: Harper & Row, 1986); Habermas quoted in Dana R. Villa, "Postmodernism and the Public Sphere," *American Political Science Review* 86 (1992): 714.

10. Kevin Mattson, *Creating a Democratic Public: The Struggle for Urban Participatory Democracy during the Progressive Era* (University Park: Pennsylvania State University Press, 1998), 4.

11. Several scholars argue that "face-to-face" encounters significantly enhance citizens' social and political engagement: Robert Lake and R. Robert Huckfeldt, "Social Capital, Social Networks, and Political Participation," *Political Psychology* 19

(1998): 567–83; R. Robert Huckfeldt and John Sprague, *Citizens, Politics, and Social Communication: Information and Influence in an Election Campaign* (Cambridge: Cambridge University Press, 1995); Robert D. Putnam, *Bowling Alone: The Collapse and Revival of American Community* (New York: Touchstone, 2000); Benjamin Barber, *Strong Democracy: Participatory Politics for a New Age* (Berkeley: University of California Press, 1984).

12. Jane Mansbridge, "Self-interest and Political Transformation," in *Reconsidering the Democratic Public*, ed. George Maces and Russell L. Harrison (University Park: Pennsylvania State University Press, 1993).

13. Benjamin Barber, *A Place for Us: How to Make Society Civil and Democracy Strong* (New York: Hill & Wang, 1998), 85.

14. M. S. Granovetter, "The Strength of Weak Ties," *American Journal of Sociology* 78 (1973): 1360–80.

15. C. Wright Mills, *White Collar: The American Middle Classes* (New York: Oxford University Press, 1951/1956), 349–50.

16. The term *micro-mobilization context* is Doug McAdam's in *Freedom Summer* (New York: Oxford University Press, 1988), 134–35.

17. Putnam, *Bowling Alone*, 22, distinguishes between "bridging" social capital that reaches across sociopolitical cleavages and the perhaps less beneficial "bonding" social capital that is characterized by close-knit, insular ties.

18. Verta Taylor, "Social Movement Continuity: The Women's Movement in Abeyance," *American Sociological Review* 54 (1989): 761–75.

19. Taylor, "Social Movement Continuity."

20. Maryann Barakso, "Membership Influence in Large Voluntary Associations," paper presented at the Annual Meeting of the Southern Political Science Association, Savannah, Ga., November 6–9, 2002.

21. Michael W. Foley and Bob Edwards, "Is It Time to Disinvest in Social Capital?" *Journal of Public Policy* 19 (1999): 219–31.

22. Foley and Edwards, "Time to Disinvest?"

23. John D. McCarthy and Mark Wolfson, "Resource Mobilization by Local Social Movement Organizations: The Role of Agency, Strategy, and Structure," *American Sociological Review* 61 (1996): 1070–88.

24. Robert Michels, *Political Parties: A Sociological Study of the Oligarchical Tendencies of Modern Democracy* (New York: Collier, 1962); Seymour Martin Lipset, Martin A. Trow, and James S. Coleman, *Union Democracy: The Internal Politics of the International Typographical Union* (New York: Free Press, 1956).

25. See Jack Walker, *Mobilizing Interest Groups in America* (Ann Arbor: University of Michigan Press, 1991); Theda Skocpol, *Protecting Soldiers and Mothers: The Political Origins of Social Policy in the United States* (Cambridge: Harvard University Press, 1992); Margaret Weir, *Politics and Jobs: The Boundaries of Employment Policy in the United States* (Princeton: Princeton University Press, 1992); Sven Steinmo, Kathleen Thelen, and Frank Longstreth, eds., *Structuring Politics: Historical Institutionalism in Comparative Analysis* (Cambridge: Cambridge University Press, 1992); and John W. Kingdon, *Agendas, Alternatives, and Public Policies*, 2d ed. (New York: Harper Collins, 1995).

NOW Documents Cited

All documents, unless noted otherwise, are archived at Schlesinger Library, Radcliffe College, Harvard University, National Organization for Women Collection.

Articles

Alexander, Dolores. "The Women's Movement: A Unique Revolution Demanding a Unique Ideology for NOW." *NOW Acts*, January 1970.

"Chapter News." *NOW Acts*, May 1968.

"Congressional Sponsors Take New Initiative in Campaign." *National NOW Times*, April 1982, 1.

"Connecting Grassroots Activists and NOW Action Center a Priority." *National NOW Times*, Winter 1999. http://www.now.org/nnt/winter-99/activists.html.

DeCrow, Karen. "Call to Philadelphia Conference." *Do It NOW*, May/June 1975.

———. "The First Women's State of the Union Address." Delivered by NOW President Karen DeCrow on January 13, 1977, at George Washington University, Washington, D.C.

"Democratic Rules Committee to Offer Strong 'Equal Division' Proposals." *National NOW Times*, August 1980, 4.

Do It NOW. January/February 1975.

Do It NOW. March/April 1975.

"Dollars and Sense of Revolution." *NOW Acts* 3 (Winter 1970).

"ERA Countdown Ends: Spurs Renewed Fight for Equality." *National NOW Times*, August 1982, 1.

"ERA Supporters Win Major Victories in NC Primaries." *National NOW Times*, August 1982, 4.

"Feminists Display Clout at Democratic Convention." *National NOW Times*, September 1980, 1, 4.

Goldsmith, Judy. "PAC/Woman Walk to Raise Funds for Feminist Candidates." *National NOW Times*, August 1982, 5.

"Goldsmith Speech to 1982 NOW Conference." *National NOW Times*, October 1982, 2.

Goodman, Ellen. "At Large." *National NOW Times*, November 1981, 5.

Harris, Louis. "ERA Support Soars as Deadline Nears." *National NOW Times*, June/July 1982, 3.

"Highlights of NOW's National Membership Conference, December 7–8, 1968 in Atlanta." *NOW Acts*, 1969.

Ireland, Patricia. "Clinton, Our Option, Not Our Answer." *National NOW Times*, November 1996.

"Mega-Membership Drive Amplifies NOW's Voice; Payoff Includes Prizes—and New Members." *National NOW Times*, March 1997.

"Membership Contest Increases Activist Ranks." *National NOW Times*, October 1997. http://www.now.org/nnt/10–97/memb.html.

NOW, http://www.now.org/nnt/11-96/elex.html.

NOW, http://www.now.org/nnt/11-96/elex.html.

NOW, http://www.now.org/nnt/fall-98/elect.html.

NOW, http://www.now.org/nnt/fall-98/elect.html.

NOW, http://www.now.org/nnt/winter-99/electns.html.

NOW, http://www.now.org/nnt/winter-99/electns.html.

NOW, http://www.now.org.nnt.03-97/mega.html.

NOW, http://www.now.org/nnt/05-97/megamemb.html.

NOW, http://www.now.org/organiza/computer.html.

NOW Acts. March 1969.

"NOW Conferences Make History." 1979 National NOW Conference Book.

"NOW PACs Seek $3 Million to Fight Right Wing Assault." *National NOW Times*, September 1982, 2.

"NOW Statements and Articles on Allegations against President Clinton." http://www.now.org/issues/harass/clinton.html.

"NOW Statements and Articles on Jones vs. Clinton." http://www.now.org/issues/harass/jones.html.

NOW, "Technological Equipment and Service Needs." http://www.now.org/nnt/fall-99/pac.html.

"NOW Vows New Campaign to Win ERA." *National NOW Times*, March 1983, 1.

"A President with a Pragmatic Approach." *National NOW Times*, October 1982, 3.

"Prizes Added to Mega-Membership Drive: Extra Incentives Boost Participation." *National NOW Times*, May 1997.

"Republicans Block Equality for Women." *National NOW Times*, March 1982.

Richards, Clay F. "Women Seen as Major Political Force." *National NOW Times*, April 1982, 1, 6.

"Right-Wing Victory Claims Distorted." *National NOW Times*, December/January 1980–81, 1, 5.

Roth, Sandy, and Lillian Waugh. "Pro Statement, Proposed NOW Bylaws." October 17, 1976.

Saffy, Edna. *Do It NOW*. January/February 1975.

"The Significance of the Democratic Convention." *National NOW Times*, September 1980, 7.

"Statement of NOW President Patricia Ireland Calling for Fair Treatment of Jones' Suit, Questioning Right Wing's Disingenuous Fervor." May 6, 1994. http://www.now.org/issues/harass/jones.html.

Taylor, Paul. "NOW Seeking $3 Million War Chest to Oust ERA Foes, Fight New Right." *National NOW Times*, September 1982, 6.
"Teams Come Forward for 1993 Election." *National NOW Times*, June 1993.
"Unprecedented Numbers of Women File in Florida State Races Post-ERA." *National NOW Times*, August 1982, 1.
Wells-Schooley, Jane. "Reagan Leads Republican Assault on Abortion, Birth Control." *National NOW Times*, August 1982, 1.
"Window on Washington." *National NOW Times*, September 1982, 2.
"Women Vote Differently than Men: Feminist Bloc Emerges in 1980 Elections," *National NOW Times*, December/January 1980–81, 1.
"Women Weren't Born Democrat, Republican, or Yesterday." *National NOW Times*, October 1982, 7.
"Yes, Ronnie, There Really Is a Gender Gap!" *National NOW Times*, November/December 1982, 7.

Letters

Betty Friedan to Alice Rossi. March 1, 1967.
——. September 20, 1967.
——. October 12, 1966.
——. October 20, 1967.
Jo Ann Evans Gardner to Gene Kolb. December 11, 1973.
Ireland, Patricia. "Letter from Patricia Ireland to the Media about Portrayal of NOW." April 1998. http://www.now.org/press/04–98/letter-ed.html.
Fran Kolb to Wilma Scott Heide. December 11, 1973.
Alice Rossi to Betty Friedan. August 23, 1966.
Alice Rossi to potential members. September 1, 1966.
Alice S. Rossi to Dr. Kathryn F. Clarenbach. October 4, 1966.
——. December 13, 1966.
——. November 9, 1966.
Seattle Ad Hoc Committee to National Board. March 13, 1975.
Eleanor Smeal to attendees. National NOW Conference Book, 1980.

Memoranda

Martha Buck and Mary Anne Sedey to National NOW Officers and Board Members. March 22, 1976.
Kathryn F. Clarenbach to Board of Directors. June 14, 1967.
Kathryn F. Clarenbach to NOW Chapter Conveners and Presidents, re: Legal Defense. May 23, 1968.
Karen DeCrow to Politics Task Force, National Officers and Board Members, Chapter Presidents and Conveners. June 26, 1972.
Betty Friedan to All Board Members. January 24, 1967.
Chris Guerrero to National Board Members. April 3, 1976.
"An Invitation to Join." National Organization for Women, August 1966.
Beverly Jones, Chair of Board Organization Committee, to National Board. January 1976.
Esther Kaw, Vice President of Public Relations, to National NOW Board of Directors. April 3, 1976.
Legislative Task Force, Florida State Legislative Coordinator, to NOW Board Members. March 8, 1976.

"Memorandum to All Political Parties." January 17, 1974.
Jan Pittman-Liebman, Legislative Vice President, and Casey Hughes, Director of Legislative Office, to NOW National Board of Directors. July 23, 1975.
Charlene Suneson to Board of Directors. October 12, 1973.

National Meetings: Minutes, Resolutions, Summaries, and Transcripts

"1980 Conference Resolutions, 1980 Presidential Elections." *National NOW Times*, October/November 1980.
"1980 Conference Resolutions, Equal Division." *National NOW Times*, October/November 1980.
"1981 Conference Resolutions, ERA." *National NOW Times*, October 1981.
"1981 Conference Resolutions, Political Action for Reproductive Rights." October 1981.
"1982 Conference Resolutions, Feminist Consciousness Raising Resolution." *National NOW Times*, October 1982, 4.
"1995 National NOW Conference Resolutions." http://www.now.org/organization/conference/1995/resoluti.html.
Minutes of the Organizing Conference. National Organization for Women (NOW), Saturday, October 29, 1966.
——. NOW National Board Meeting, October 29, 1966.
——. NOW National Board Meeting, November 27–28, 1968.
——. NOW National Board Meeting, March 29–30, 1969.
——. NOW National Board Meeting, December 6, 1969.
——. NOW National Board Meeting, May 2–3, 1970.
——. NOW National Board Meeting, February 1974.
——. NOW National Board Meeting, July 1975.
——. NOW National Board Meeting, April 1976.
——. NOW National Board Minutes, July 30–31, 1977.
——. NOW National Board Meeting, February 1978.
——. NOW National Board Meeting, February 1983.
National Conference Book, 1983.
"Revolution: Tomorrow Is NOW." No date. [1973?]
"Summary of National Board Meeting, December 4–5, 1982." *National NOW Times*, November/December 1982, 11.
"Summary of National Board Meeting, December 4–5, 1982." *National NOW Times*, November/December 1982, 11.
"Summary of National Board Meeting: April 24–26, 1981." *National NOW Times*, September 1981, 15.
"Summary of National Board Meetings: October 2, 1980." *National NOW Times*, October/November 1980, 23.
Transcript, National NOW Conference, 1978.
Transcript, National NOW Conference, April 22–24, 1977, Sunday, April 24, a.m. and p.m. sessions.

Policies and Bylaws

"National Organization for Women Policy Manual: Administration," 1979.
"National Organization for Women Policy Manual: Issues," 1979.
NOW Bylaws, as amended, 1996.

Reports and Addresses

Address, Toni Carabillo, "Power Is the Name of the Game." California NOW State
   Conference in San Diego, Calif., October 28, 1973.
1997 Budget. http://www.now.org/nnt/05–97/budget.html.
"About the NOW Foundation." http://www.nowfoundation.org/about.html.
Annual Report, National Organization for Women Foundation, 1994. http://www
   .nowfoundation.org/board94.html.
"NOW, It's Money." Pamphlet, no date.
"NOW Politics Task Force Report." October 1972.
Report of Informal Meeting of NOW Members from Illinois, Indiana and Wisconsin.
   Saturday, January 21, 1967.
Report of the Legal Committee to Board and Members of NOW at First Annual Con-
   ference. Washington, D.C., November 18–19, 1967.
Report, Betty Friedan, NOW National Board Meeting Minutes, June 28–29, 1969.
Report, Betty Friedan, NOW National Board Meeting Minutes, December 6, 1969.
"Summary of Questionnaire for NOW." 1974.

Index